Abram Herbert Lewis

Biblical Teachings

Concerning the Sabbath and the Sunday

Abram Herbert Lewis

Biblical Teachings
Concerning the Sabbath and the Sunday

ISBN/EAN: 9783337719272

Printed in Europe, USA, Canada, Australia, Japan

Cover: Foto ©Lupo / pixelio.de

More available books at **www.hansebooks.com**

BIBLICAL TEACHINGS

CONCERNING

THE SABBATH

AND

THE SUNDAY,

BY

A. H. LEWIS, D. D.

AUTHOR OF "SABBATH AND SUNDAY, ARGUMENT AND HISTORY"; "A CRITICAL HISTORY OF THE SABBATH AND THE SUNDAY, IN THE CHRISTIAN CHURCH;' "A CRITICAL HISTORY OF SUNDAY LEGISLATION FROM 321 TO 1888, A. D.;" "THE SEVENTH-DAY BAPTIST HAND BOOK." EDITOR OF "THE OUTLOOK AND SABBATH QUARTERLY," AND OF "THE LIGHT OF HOME."

TO WHICH IS ADDED AN IMPORTANT CHAPTER ON
"THE ORIGIN OF THE WEEK."

Second Edition, Revised.

THE AMERICAN SABBATH TRACT SOCIETY :
ALFRED CENTRE, N. Y.
1888.

PREFACE.

In 1870 the author of the following pages issued a work entitled "The Sabbath and the Sunday, Argument and History." The favorable reception granted to that volume, and the increasing agitation concerning the Sabbath question in the United States, led to the issue of three other volumes, as follows: The first edition of this book in 1884; "A Critical History of the Sabbath and the Sunday in The Christian Church," a larger volume, which embodies the history of the theories and practices relative to both days; in 1886, "A Critical History of Sunday Legislation, from A. D. 321 to 1888," which appeared in March, 1888.

The second edition of this book appears at a time when the agitation of the Sabbath question is more wide-spread and intense than at any previous time in our national history. The popular tendency is to avoid a direct appeal to the Word of God in the settlement of the question. There is also a persistent but most unscholarly effort made in certain circles to avoid the claims of the Sabbath as against the Sunday, by asserting that the week is an uncertain and variable division of time, and that we cannot attain any definite knowledge as to what day is the Sabbath. The following pages exalt the Word of God as the *only rule of faith and practice* for Christian men.

The Sabbath question is larger than any denominational lines. It involves the highest interests and the future destiny of the Christian Church. The theory which seeks to abolish the Decalogue, and thus remove the Sabbath, is illogical, deceptive and destructive. Few men professing to be Christians could urge such a theory were it not for their desire to avoid the claims of the Sabbath. The mission of this book is to exalt the truth that Calvary glorifies Sinai, but does not remove it; that faith in Christ *establishes* the law of God, but does not make it *void*.

Truth can afford to wait calmly, while error digs its own grave. But for the sake of truth we have the right to demand a candid and earnest investigation of the Sabbath question from the Biblical standpoint. What saith God's Word? Read thoughtfully, and act in the light of truth and in the presence of God, from whose eyes neither excuses nor sophistry can hide the soul.

PLAINFIELD, N. J., June, 1888.

THE SABBATH AND THE SUNDAY.

CHAPTER I.

A PRIORI ARGUMENT.

The patterns of all things must exist as pure thoughts in the mind of Jehovah before there can be any outward creation. These pattern thoughts are the laws by which the work of creation is developed, and governed. Therefore "law" in its pure primary meaning is another name for *God's ideal.* Hence no primary law can be abrogated or changed; for God's ideals are perfect and absolute. Any change or abrogation of primary laws must destroy the creation, or the government which has been developed according to those laws, and is founded upon them. Abrogate the law of "gravitation," and the physical universe is at once destroyed. The same is true in moral government. Even the disobedience of a single subject produces discord, and to a certain extent, breaks up the order of the government. If the law-making power shall change or abrogate the laws on which the government rests, the government is changed or destroyed. It is also a self-evident truth that all primary laws must antedate the government which is based upon them, and all perfect laws must meet the necessities which grow out of the relations between the governor and the governed. Obedience on the part of the governed is at once the sign of fealty, and the means of blessing.

It is befitting to inquire, in the light of the foregoing principles, whether the Sabbath Law is a primary law in moral government, or only a temporary enactment made with reference to a primary law.

The commemorative rest of Jehovah at the close of his creative work is the first expression of the Sabbath idea. This rest follows close upon the completion of the work, as though it were a part of the original pattern. And when it is remembered that the Sabbath law meets the demands which grow out of our relations to God, which relations existed from the birth of the race, the conclusion is inevitable that the Sabbath law was a primary, structural law in the moral universe, and, like all other primary laws, had its origin in the mind of Jehovah "before the world was."

The idea of God as *Creator* is the all-embracing idea. His character as Law-giver, and Redeemer, flows from the idea of Creator. Fealty to God, as well as our highest good, demands that we constantly remember him and our relations to him. Hence the Sabbath law links itself with this all-embracing idea of the true God, the maker of heaven and of earth, the Creator and Redeemer of men, and holds it ever before us. A law which thus forms the central thread of communion between the Creator and the creature, which thus meets the universal demands arising from our relations to him, which is God's never-ceasing representative in time, must be as universal and enduring as the system of which it is a part.

Man is a social as well as a religious being. In this dual nature the highest motive that can enter into our relations to each other is, "Love to man." This unites the race, and linking with "Love to God" leads us up to him. The universal expression of love to God is worship. Social worship is, therefore, the natural result of the highest action of man's dual nature. But social worship could never become universal or permanent without a stated and definite time, fixed by the author of man's nature and the object of his worship. Illustration: If a governor orders an election of officers, and appoints no time when the election shall be held, there is not only a want of wisdom in the arrangement, but the election must be a failure. To say that God did not pre-ordain the Sabbath law, as a structural law in moral government, is to charge the Perfect One with similar folly.

Thus it is seen that God's relations to his own work, our relations to him, and our relations to each other, all combine to show that the Sabbath law must have been a primary, structural law of the moral government under which we exist. Being such, it can only be abrogated by the annulling of all these relations, and the destruction of the government.

CHAPTER II.

SCRIPTURAL ARGUMENT.

Approaching the Scriptures, we find the fundamental facts in exact harmony with the foregoing *a priori* conclusions. When the Sabbath law appears, it is linked with the beginning of man's experience, and founded upon the example of Jehovah.

Hence the question arises at the threshold of the Scriptural argument concerning the Sabbath:

Can the Law of the Sabbath and the Day of the Sabbath be separated? Two points carefully examined, will answer this question.

(*a*) Why was the seventh day chosen as the Sabbath?

(*b*) By virtue of what did it become the Sabbath?

(*a*) God could not commemorate the work of creation until it was completed. It was not completed until the close of the sixth day. Hence no day previous to the seventh could have been chosen as the Sabbath. Previous to the seventh day creation was only a "becoming." With the opening of the seventh day it sprang into full being. This, therefore, was creation's birthday, and hence the only day that could be chosen to commemorate the rest of God from the completed work of creating. As one cannot celebrate his birthday on a day earlier or later than that on which his birth occurred, so Jehovah sanctified the seventh as the only day which could answer the original idea of the Sabbath law. Therefore the Sabbath Law and the Sabbath Day designated by its author are inseparable. Applied to any other day the law has no meaning.

(*b*) The acts of Jehovah by which the seventh day was consecrated as the Sabbath. God rested on that day, hence the sacredness arising from his example can pertain to no other day. God blessed the day and hallowed it, *because* he had rested upon it. Thus the elements of sacredness and of commemorativeness are inseparably connected with the day. If the law be applied to another day, it becomes meaningless; for the law demands a day thus made sacred, and no other day than the seventh could be made sacred for those reasons. Nor can the seventh day cease to be thus sacred, until it shall cease to be a fact that God rested upon that day and blessed it. This can never be.

Again, no other day than the seventh can meet the

demands of our own natures, since no other day can keep God in mind through this commemorative sacredness. Any other day, observed for any reason not mentioned in the law, has another language—speaks of other things, and hence cannot speak to the soul as God designed the Sabbath should speak. Thus it appears that God chose the seventh day for good and sufficient reasons, reasons which spring from the eternal fitness of things, and which co-exist with our race. Therefore, if there be any Sabbath, it must be the seventh day. The *law* centers around the *day*, and is meaningless when applied to any other. Much is said by certain writers concerning the "Sabbath institution," as though it were distinct from the Sabbath law and the Sabbath day. A glance will suffice to show the illogicalness of such a claim. An institution is only the outgrowth of organific law. Refuse or neglect to obey the law the institution is destroyed. Illustration: During the late "rebellion," the institutions of the United States' government ceased to exist wherever the laws of that government were disobeyed. So he who refuses to obey the Sabbath law destroys the Sabbath institution so far as his power extends.

At this point, some readers will raise the query as to the length of God's creative days, and their bearing on the question before us. Our answer, briefly, is this: God's power is infinite, measureless. His acts, and the time in which he performs them, are also unmeasurable by us. We apprehend that the creative week was infinitely longer than our week of seven days of twenty-four hours. But since it was a week, and since God rested from his work on the seventh day of that week, and since he commanded us *to do in our week, as he did in his*, all difficulty in the case vanishes. Our week is modeled after God's by his command. We are to do in our sphere of action after his example in his sphere of action. The Sabbath law, given by him, demands this, and the observance of any other day than the seventh and last day of the week, for any reason, is not obedience to God's law. Finite men, acting in finite days, do follow the example of an Infinite God, acting in unmeasured days, *if they preserve the same order*, according to his command; otherwise, they do not.

The second question is: *Was the Sabbath Law known to men before the giving of the Decalogue at Mount Sinai?* All the arguments presented in a former chapter, to prove that the Sabbath law is a primary law, will apply with equal force to the above question. To those reasons the following may be added: All the primary relations between God and his creatures existed before the giving of the Decalogue. All the wants of man's nature existed during that time, hence all laws made to meet these relations and answer these wants must have been coexistent with the relations and demands. There was an especial demand for a knowledge of the Sabbath during this period, as a safeguard against the prevailing tendency to forget God and accept heathenism. Besides this, God having made the Sabbath sacred at creation, it could have been no less than sin to profane it in any time thereafter, and God does not leave his creatures without the knowledge requisite to obedience. Hence we must conclude that the Sabbath was known before the giving of the law at Sinai. This conclusion is in harmony with the unanswerable argument of Paul in the Epistle to the Romans,[1] in which he shows that since sin existed "from Adam to Moses," therefore the law must have existed, for "Sin is not imputed where there is no law." Christ proclaims the same truth when he teaches the eternal nature of the law, and the fact that "the Sabbath was made for man, and not man for the Sabbath."[2] In this Christ clearly indicates that the Sabbath law antedated the race, and was given for the especial ben-

---

[1] Romans v. 12—15; and iv. 15.
[2] Mark ii. 27.

efit of the race. Hence also his right, as "Lord of the Sabbath," to indicate how it ought to be observed, since all things were made by him.

The brief Scriptural record concerning the period between the creation and the giving of the law confirms the foregoing conclusions. In the second chapter of Genesis, first to fourth verses, we have the history of the instituting of the Sabbath in the following words:

"And the heaven and the earth were finished and all the host of them."

"And on the seventh day God finished his work which he had made; and he rested on the seventh day from all his work which he had made."

"And God blessed the seventh day and hallowed it; because that in it he rested from all his work which God created and made.[1]"

This fact so full of deep meaning, and inseparable from the history of creation, could not have been unknown to Adam and the patriarchs who "walked with God," and were taught by him. Knowing of the existence of the Sabbath, they must have known of its sacredness, and their duty to observe it. The septenary division of time into weeks was well understood during the patriarchal age.[2] This knowl-

[1] All quotations are from the Revised Version.
[2] See Genesis vii. 4—8; 10—12.

edge necessitates a knowledge of the Sabbath by which the weeks are separated.[1] But positive testimony is not wanting. The sixteenth chapter of Exodus shows that the Sabbath was known and observed before the giving of the Decalogue at Sinai, and that the first special test of obedience which God made after the Israelites left Egypt was concerning its observance. The giving of the manna occured on the fifteenth day of the second month, and the Hebrews did not reach Sinai until some time during the third month after their departure from Egypt. In the fourth verse of this 16th of Exodus, it is said that God told Moses:

"Behold I will rain bread from heaven for you, and the people shall go out and gather a day's portion every day, that I may prove them, whether they will walk in my law or no."

This shows that the test of obedience was to be made in connection with the gathering of the manna according to a certain *daily rate*.

The next verse gives the test, viz.:

"And it shall come to pass, on the sixth day that they shall prepare that which they bring in, and it shall be twice as much as they gather daily."

[1] For collateral testimony showing that the week and the Sabbath were known also outside the patriarchal line, testimony which indicates an universal revelation concerning the week and the Sabbath at the first, see Appendix A.

It is plain that the test lay in the *voluntary preparations* for the Sabbath on the part of the people; for in the *sixteenth* verse Moses reveals nothing to the people except the order to gather the stated portion each day; and when some would not heed this order,[1] the manna not only became worthless, but Moses testified his displeasure at their disobedience. The people were not ordered to gather a double portion on the sixth day, nor were they at first informed that the manna should not fall upon the Sabbath. They were left wholly ignorant on this point in order that the test of their obedience might be complete. Hence it is said in the *twenty-second* verse that when the sixth day came, and the people voluntarily gathered an extra portion for the Sabbath, the rulers came at once and told Moses of their apparent disobedience. Then, for the first time, Moses revealed to them what God had said concerning the test to be made and told them[2] that there should be no manna on the Sabbath. Nevertheless some went out to seek for it on the Sabbath, and God rebuked them in a way, and with a severity, which is wholly inconsistent with the idea that this was their first offense. He says:[3]

"*How long refuse ye to keep my commandments*

[1] 20th verse.   [2] 26th verse.   [3] 28th verse.

and my laws," etc. There is no appearance of anything new, or of the introduction of anything before unknown. The conditions of the test, and the voluntary act of the people in preparing for the Sabbath, show that the law of the Sabbath was well understood by them, and that it had come to them from the patriarchal age, before their bondage in Egypt.

GIVING THE LAW.

A careful study of the history of the organization of the Jewish nation reveals the following important facts:

1. The Decalogue was given first in order of time, as the embodiment of all moral law, the foundation of all government.

2. Certain ceremonies were instituted teaching physical and spiritual purity, offering forgiveness through faith and obedience, and pointing to a coming Saviour.

3. Civil and ecclesiastico-civil regulations were made for the organization of the nation and the enforcement of obedience to the laws of the Decalogue, which by its nature, and by the circumstances that attended the giving of it, is shown to be entirely distinct from the ceremonial and civil regulations. That nine of these ten laws are eternal is unques-

tioned. Some are found who claim that the Sabbath law, embodied in the fourth commandment is ceremonial and not moral. If the claim be true, then God, the infinite in wisdom, placed it where it *did not belong*, and so deceived, not only the Israelites, but the world. By such misplacement, too, the ceremonial code was left imperfect, in a very important particular. It is also an unquestioned fact that the Jews never deemed the Sabbath law as ceremonial. God bases the Sabbath law upon his own example, and teaches that it finds its beginning and authority in his acts at the close of the creative week; while, if the above claim be true, it was *not* commemorative of God and his work, but typical of Christ. A theory which thus charges God with ignorance or premeditated deception, or with both, sinks under the weight of its own inconsistency.

THE TWO COVENANTS.

Before closing this chapter, it is necessary to answer another query which will arise concerning what are loosely called the Old and the New Covenants. It is a prominent part of the stock in trade of modern No-Sabbathists to claim that God made one covenant with the Jews, which was annulled when Christ came, and that thus the Decalogue, and so the Sabbath law, were annulled. The confusion which exists in the popular theories on this point is great. It arises from a superficial understanding of the nature of God's government, and the meaning of the term covenant. To clear up this confusion, it is necessary to inquire what the meaning of covenant is, as used in the Scriptures.

Worcester gives the following excellent definition of the theological use of the term, viz.: "The promise of God to man that he shall receive certain temporal or spiritual blessings upon certain conditions, or upon the performance of the duties pointed out in the Old and New Testaments."

What was the "old covenant"? The term covenant occurs first in Gen. vi. 18, in connection with the building of the Ark; that covenant was essentially this: Noah, believing God's word, and building the Ark, as God directed, should be saved from destruction. This is the model of all "covenants." Men are to do a given thing, whereupon God does or grants certain things, as results. The covenant with Abraham, Gen. xv., is of the same nature; in this, God promises to give "This land," etc. (18 v.), to Abraham's seed, if they obey him. In the 17th chapter the promise of a great posterity is added. In all the covenants between individuals, the same features appear; an agreement wherein each has a part to perform. When the children of Israel groaned under the bondage in Egypt, God assured them that he remembered his promise to give them the land of Canaan. Ex. ii. 24; vi. 4, 5.

In the organizing of the Hebrew theocracy, after the exodus, the deeper meaning of covenant comes out, in what is properly termed the law covenant. Man is not an independent contracting party, but a subject who is under obligation to obey whatever God may command. Hence, obedience to God's law is the only way in which man can keep a covenant with God. In Exod. xix. 5, 6, obedience is the ground on which it is promised that Israel shall become a "kingdom of priests and an holy nation." Since the law of God contains the essential terms of the covenant by indicating what obedience consists in, the law is often spoken of as the covenant, by a common figure, metonymy. This metonymical use of law, and covenant, is common in Exodus, and in Deuteronomy. The failure to recognize this use has led to no little confusion and error, as has also the fact that the reasons assigned in Deuteronomy why the Isralites should obey the law of God, are specific, national, and narrow, when compared with the general and eternal reasons on which the laws of the

Decalogue rest. This covenant concerning the keeping of the Decalogue also included the method by which men might find forgiveness when they had broken the law, viz., by sacrifices. This was the method of "administering" the law. In the broadest sense, therefore, the "old covenant" included, (*a*) The Decalogue, which was the basis of all else. (*b*) The ceremonial system through which forgiveness of sin might be found in case of the transgression of the Decalogue.

In order to complete our answer to the query under consideration, we here add: the "new covenant" was, (*a*) The same law of God, written in men's hearts instead of on tables of stone. That is, changed from an outward restraint to an inward control; thus its power was intensified. (*b*) Forgiveness of sin—the transgression of God's law—through faith in Christ, and not through ceremonies and sacrifices.

A common and most hurtful error of our time is the essential destruction of this new covenant, by teaching the abrogation of the Decalogue, and hence the removal of all obligation from men; which, being done, there can be no covenant, since obedience is man's part of the covenant. The Epistle to the Hebrews is referred to by many as teaching such abrogation of the Decalogue, and hence of the Sabbath. Without discussing the authorship of Hebrews, it is pertinent to say that it is not a general Epistle. It is addressed to a single church, or to a small group, probably at Alexandria. Those addressed had accepted Christ as the Messiah, but still clung to the ceremonial code as the ground of forgiveness and justification. Thus they were sure to sink back into Judaism, unless they could be brought to a higher view of faith in Christ, as both Messiah and Saviour. The first ten chapters of Hebrews aim to bring about this broader view, and this deeper conviction. The argument culminates in the sixteenth verse of the tenth chapter, wherein the new covenant shows the law written in men's hearts, and forgiveness granted through the blood of Christ. The argument is not that the law is done away, but that, under the gospel covenant, men are made free from the sin resulting from disobedience, through Christ's sacrificial work, and not through the offerings whereby forgiveness had been sought under Judaism.

The same idea is brought out in Paul's second letter to the Corinthians (iii. 2-11). This is often adduced as showing the abrogation of the Decalogue, whereas the true intent is a comparison of the glory of the two methods of administering the law, and finding forgiveness for its transgression. In the sixth verse, Paul defines the new covenant as based upon the deeper, spiritual meaning of the law. In the seventh verse he shows that the law of the Decalogue, even when written on stones, was glorious, but when it is written in the heart, and its deeper meaning is understood, it is far more glorious. The eleventh verse shows that what is specifically spoken of as being "done away," is the glory which shone on the face of Moses when the law was given on Sinai. This represents the glory of the former method of administering the law, which glory passed away before the surpassing glory of the gospel method of administering the same law. It is the same thought which is set forth in Hebrews, by the law as written on tables of stone, as less powerful than when written in men's hearts by the Holy Spirit.

Paul to the Romans teaches the same truth in the most intense manner. The first seven chapters of Romans are terrible in the severity with which they set forth the power of the law of God, the Decalogue, whereby comes the knowledge of sin, and its condemnation. At the same time they set forth faith in Christ as the means of relief from this condemnation, through forgiveness. The argument opens in the 16th verse of the 1st chapter. It reaches the climax in the 7th chapter. But lest any should misapprehend his meaning, Paul draws several clear-cut conclusions in the course of the argument. He places the main question at rest, and beyond controversy, in the 3d chapter, 31st verse, "Do we then make void the law through faith? God forbid. Yea, we establish the law." The logic of this proposition is unmistakable. Faith is demanded under the gospel as the means of salvation from sin; hence faith establishes the law which convicts of sin. This is the burden of Paul's argument throughout. "For by the law is the knowledge of sin;" "For where no law is, there is no transgression;" "But sin is not imputed where there is no law;" "What then? shall we sin because we are not under the law but under grace? God forbid;" "What shall we say then? Is the law sin? God forbid, Nay I had not known sin but by the law;" "Wherefore the law is holy, and the commandment holy, and just and good." Rom. iii. 20; iv. 15; v. 13; vi. 15; vii. 7, 12. Such are the conclusions which Paul scatters through his argument before he reaches the climax in the seventh chapter. Please study those chapters, and see that the whole economy of grace in the gospel is a farce, if we attempt to interpret Paul's argument in any other way. If the Decalogue, the only law which can convict of sin, be abrogated by the death of Christ, or destroyed as a part of the old covenant, then Christ made it impossible for men to sin or to have a knowledge of sin after that time. Thus he died to redeem men from that which could not be. To such contradiction does no-lawism come. Paul taught that the law of God which convicts of sin, the Decalogue, was in full authority, as a condemning power. We have already seen that the author of Hebrews teaches that the law is intensified in its authority and power to condemn, by being written in men's hearts. Thus Christ who came not to destroy the law, and the apostle who teaches that it is established, confirmed, strengthened by faith, agree.

The Decalogue instead of being done away as a part of the Old Covenant, is the foundation of both covenants, being the rule whereby man is to be guided in keeping his part of the covenant with God. Upon the ground of obedience God promised Israel certain blessings. But in his mercy he also added a method whereby forgiveness might be attained in case of failure to obey. Under the Jewish economy this was through the ceremonial system; under the Gospel it is through faith in Christ: under both systems confession must precede forgiveness, which must also be followed by a forsaking of sin in order to continued acceptance. When Christ came the better method of finding forgiveness and salvation from sin superseded that which was more burdensome and less glorious. The foundation of both covenants was God's law in the Decalogue. The difference between the two was in the method by which men were to find forgiveness in case of transgression.

CHAPTER III.

TEACHINGS OF CHRIST CONCERNING THE LAW.

Christ is the central figure in both dispensations. If new expressions of the Father's will are to be made in connection with the work of Christ on earth, they must be made by the "Immanuel," who is thus "reconciling the world unto himself." Did Christ teach the abrogation of the Decalogue of which the Sabbath law is a part? Let his own words answer:

"Think not that I came to destroy the law or the prophets. I came not to destroy, but to fulfill. For verily I say unto you, till heaven and earth pass away, one jot or one tittle shall in no wise pass away from the law, till all things be accomplished. Whosoever, therefore, shall break one of these least commandments, and shall teach men so, shall be called least in the kingdom of heaven; but whosoever shall do and teach them, he shall be called great in the kingdom of heaven."[1]

When Christ speaks of the law ($\tau\grave{o}\nu$ $\nu\acute{o}\mu o\nu$) in these emphatic words, he cannot mean the ceremonial code, for these ceremonies were typical of him

[1] Matthew v. 17—19.

and must pass away with his death. Besides this, the word fulfill (πληρῶσαι) means the opposite of destruction (καταλῦσαι). Christ fulfilled the law by perfect obedience to it. He corrected false interpretations, and intensified its claims. He taught obedience to it in the spirit as well as the letter, and urged obedience from love rather than fear. Such a work could not have been done in connection with the dying ceremonies of the Jewish system. Such a work Christ did do with reference to the Decalogue. In connection with the passage above quoted Christ immediately refers to two laws from the Decalogue, explains and enforces their meaning in a way far more broad and deep than those who listened to him were wont to conceive of them.

On another occasion[1] a certain shrewd lawyer sought to entrap the Saviour by asking " which is the greatest commandment in the law." The question has no meaning unless it be applied to the Decalogue. Christ's answer includes all the commandments of the Decalogue and thus avoids the trap designed by the questioner, who sought to lead him into some distinction between laws known to be equal in their nature and extent.

In the *sixteenth* chapter of Luke,[2] Christ again

[1] Matthew xxii. 35—40.   [2] 17th verse

affirms in the strongest language, that "It is easier for heaven and earth to pass, than one tittle of the law to fail." Language could not be plainer than that which is used in these statements.

These sentiments accord fully with the practice of Christ relative to the Sabbath. He boldly condemned the unjust requirements which the Jews had attached to the observance of it, and taught that works of mercy were to be freely done on that day; that it was made for man's good, and not his injury. But he never taught that because it was "made for man" therefore it was to be abrogated, or unsanctified. Neither did he delegate to his disciples any power to teach the abrogation of the law, or of the Sabbath. On the contrary, their representative writings contain the same clear testimony in favor of the perpetuity of the law, and show the same practical observance of the Sabbath. Paul, the great reasoner among the Apostles, after an exhaustive discussion concerning the relations between the law and the Gospel, concludes the whole matter in these words:

"Do we then make the law of none effect through faith? God forbid! Nay, we establish the law."[1]

Again in the same epistle[2] he presents a conclusive argument, starting from the axiom that "where

[1] Romans iii. 31.   [2] Romans v. 13, 14.

there is no law there is no sin." Showing that since death, which came by sin, reigned from Adam to Moses, therefore the law then existed, and, by the same reasoning that if there be no law under the gospel dispensation, there can be no sin; if no sin, then no Saviour from sin, and Christ died in vain, if by his death he destroyed the law. In another place Paul contrasts the Decalogue with the ceremonial code and declares the worthlessness of the one and the binding character of the other, in these words:

"Circumcision is nothing, and uncircumcision is nothing, but the keeping of the Commandments of God."[1]

Thus, in a plain and unequivocal way, Paul teaches as his Master taught.[2]

EXAMPLE.

The example of Christ and his apostles is in full harmony with their teachings. During Christ's life, while his disciples were with him, the Sabbath was always observed by him and them. In all his acts there is no hint that the law was to be annulled. On the contrary, Christ speaks prophetically of the Sabbath as an existing institution at the time when Jeru-

---

[1] 1. Corinthians vii. 19.

[2] Passages quoted from Paul's writings, to prove the abrogation of the law, will be fully examined in another place.

salem should be destroyed,[1] and tells his disciples to pray that their flight might not occur on that day, knowing that this destruction would not come until long after his death.

DID THE APOSTLES OBSERVE THE SABBATH?

The book of Acts is the main source of history concerning these men. It tells where they journeyed, what they preached, and what befell them. The *thirteenth* chapter[2] contains the following account:

"But they, passing through from Perga, came to Antioch of Pisidia, and they went into the synagogue on the Sabbath day, and sat down."

Being invited to speak, Paul preached to them concerning Christ, and especially concerning his death and resurrection;—a significant fact to be carefully noted and more fully examined hereafter. To say that this was done by the Apostles, as *Jews*, is to charge them with unmanly dissembling. They were Christians teaching others to become Christians. Neither did they seek the synagogue on the Sabbath simply to teach the Jews; for it is stated in this same chapter, that:

" And as they went out, they besought that these words might be spoken to them the next Sabbath. And the next

[1] Matthew xxiv. 20.   [2] 14th verse.

Sabbath almost the whole city was gathered together to hear the word of God."[1]

Pursuing the history through the next chapter, we find Paul and his companions continuing to travel from place to place, preaching and gathering churches, until the calling of the council at Jerusalem, an account of which is found in the fifteenth chapter. This council and its decisions have a direct bearing upon the question under consideration. The object of the council was to decide how far Gentile converts should be required to conform to those ordinances and ceremonies which were peculiarly Jewish. Had the Sabbath belonged to these, some reference to it could not have been avoided, since the Jews deemed it of paramount importance, and Paul and his companions had just come from a tour among the Gentiles, to whom they had taught its observance. The silence of that council concerning the Sabbath, and its decisions relative to minor questions, are evidence that the Sabbath was openly recognized and observed by all, under the universal law of the fourth commandment.

The points involved in the Jerusalem council are as follows:

(*a*) Should Gentile converts be required to sub-

[1] 42d and 44th verses.

mit to circumcision and keep the ceremonial law, as requisites to salvation? To this question the council promptly answered, No. This answer did not touch the Sabbath in any way.

(*b*) Certain things were required. But these were really outside of the ceremonial code. Idolatry and lewdness were in direct violation of the laws of the Decalogue. The eating of blood was akin to idolatry, as a species of sacrilege. The first prohibition concerning it was given to Noah. Gen. ix. 4. This was repeated and more fully explained in Lev. xvii. 10-14. In the 11th verse the reason given makes the requirement more than ceremonial, since it is based on the fact that God had made blood the *sign of atonement on the altar*. To the early Jewish converts it stood as the representative of Christ's blood so lately shed for the salvation of both Jew and Gentile. Hence James deemed it worthy to be classed with moral precepts, since sacrilege and idolatry were thus one. This council was not called for the purpose of legislation, and had no power to annul a law of the Decalogue. Its purpose was to arrange the difference between the Judaistic and the Gentile elements in the church, and to testify that salvation came by faith, and not by ceremonies which had once pointed to Christ, but were now obsolete, since Christ had come and suffered. It is a preposterous stretch of logic to claim for such a council the right to annul a law of the Decalogue. And more: if silence concerning the Sabbath, on the part of this council, indicates that it deemed the Sabbath law annulled, the same is true of all the other laws except those against idolatry and lewdness. The proposition destroys itself.

At the conclusion of this council, Paul and Silas set out in one direction, and Barnabas and Mark in another, to revisit those churches already formed, and preach the Word in other fields. The history of this tour shows the same recognition and observance of the Sabbath. It is said[1] that they came to Philippi, "the chief city of that part of Macedonia, and abode there certain days," and, in the words of the historian:

"And on the Sabbath day, we went forth without the gate by a river side, where we supposed there was a place of prayer; and we sat down and spake unto the women which were come together."

This was a place for out-door worship in a city which was probably destitute of a synagogue. It was twenty years after Christ's resurrection, and among those who, of all others, would be most likely

[1] Acts xvi. 12, 13.

to discard the Sabbath. From Philippi the apostles proceeded to Thessalonica,

"Where was a synagogue of the Jews, and " Paul," as his custom was, went in unto them, and for three Sabbath days reasoned with them from the Scriptures."

" Opening and alleging that it behooved the Christ to suffer and to rise again from the dead, and that this Jesus whom said he I proclaim unto you is the Christ."

" And some of them were persuaded, and consorted with Paul and Silas; and of the devout Greeks a great multitude, and of the chief women not a few."[1]

Passing from thence to Berea, and thence to Athens, in both of which places Paul taught in the synagogues, they came to Corinth, where Paul remained "a year and six months, and reasoned in the synagogue every Sabbath, and persuaded the Jews and the Greeks."[2,3]

The nineteenth chapter relates that Paul taught for two years and three months at Ephesus. "So that all they which dwelt in Asia heard the word of the Lord Jesus, both Jews and Greeks."

[1] Acts xvii. 2, 5.
[2] Acts xviii. 4 and 11.
[3] It was at this time that Paul organized the church at Corinth, to which he wrote five years later, telling them to lay by their gifts for the poor at Jerusalem, on the first day of the week. See an examination of this passage in the next chapter.

SUMMARY.

Collating these facts, and summing up the case as regards the example of Christ and his apostles, it stands as follows:

1. During the life of Christ the Sabbath was always observed by him, and by his followers. He corrected the errors and false notions which were held concerning it, but gave no hint that it was to be abrogated.

2. The book of *Acts* gives a connected history of the recognition and observance of the Sabbath by the apostles while they were organizing many of the churches spoken of in the New Testament. These references extend over a period of eight or nine years, the last of them being at least twenty years after the resurrection.

3. In all the history of the doings and teachings of the apostles, there is not the remotest reference to the abrogation of the Sabbath.

Had there been any change made or beginning to be made, or any authority for the abrogation of the Sabbath law, the apostles must have known it. To claim that there was is therefore to charge them with studiously *concealing the truth*. And also, with recognizing and calling a day the Sabbath which *was not the Sabbath*.

Add to these considerations the following facts:

(*a*) The latest books of the New Testament, including the Gospel of John, were written about the year ninety-five. In none of these is there any trace of the change of the Sabbath, nor is the abrogation of the Sabbath law taught in them.

(*b*) The Sabbath is mentioned in the New Testament sixty times, and always in its appropriate character.

Thus the law and the gospel are in harmony, and teach that "the seventh day is the Sabbath of the Lord thy God."

But some will say, "Christ and his apostles did all this as Jews, simply." If this be true, then Christ lived and taught simply as a *Jew* and not as the *Saviour of the world*. On the contrary he was at war with the false and extravagant notions of Judaism concerning questions of truth and duty. If Christ were not a "Christian," but a "Jew," what becomes of the system which he taught? If his first followers, who periled all for him and sealed their faith with their blood, were only Jews, or worse, were dissemblers, doing that which Christians ought not to do, for sake of policy, where shall Christians be found? The assumption dies of its own inconsistency. More than this, New Testament history repeatedly states that the Greeks were taught on the Sabbath the same as the Jews, and in those churches where the Greek element predominated there is no trace of any different teaching or custom on this point. The Jewish Christians kept up their *national* institutions, for a time, such as circumcision and the passover, while all Christians accepted the Sabbath as a part of the law of God. The popular outcry against the Sabbath as "Jewish" savors more of prejudice and ignorance than of consistency and charity. Christ was in all respects, as regards nationality, a Jew. So were all the writers of the Old Testament, and all the writers of the New Testament. God has given the world no word of inspiration in the Bible, from Gentile pen, or Gentile lips. Is the Bible therefore "Jewish"? The Sabbath, if possible, is less Jewish than the Bible. It had its beginning long before a Jew was born. It is God's day marked by his own example, and sanctified by his blessing, for the race of man, beginning when the race began, and can end only when the race shall cease to exist. Christ recognized it under the gospel as he recognized each of the other eternal laws with which it is associated in the Decalogue; recognized them as the everlasting words of his Father, whose law he came to magnify and fulfill. It tells of pitiable weakness, and unchristian irreverence, to attempt to thrust out and stigmatize any part of God's truth as " Jewish," when all of God's promises and all Bible truth have come to us through the Hebrew nation.

CHAPTER IV.

OPPOSING THEORIES EXAMINED.

NO-SABBATH THEORY.

By this is meant the prevalent theory that there is no sacred time under the gospel dispensation; that the Sabbath was only a Jewish institution, which began with the Hebrew nation, and was abrogated at the death of Christ. Against such a theory the following points have already been established.

1. The Sabbath law, being a primary law in moral government, is necessarily co-existent with that government.

2. The Sabbath as God's memorial, his monument and representative in time, came into being when he rested upon the seventh day, and blessed and sanctified it.

3. The Sabbath law grew out of the relations which always have existed between the Creator and the creature, and meet certain universal demands in human life; it cannot therefore cease until these relations and demands shall cease.

4. The Bible history, and collateral testimony, (see appendix,) show that the Sabbath was observed previous to the organization of the Hebrew nation.

5. When Jehovah gave the eternal laws of his government to the world, in the Decalogue, he placed the Sabbath law as the key-stone of the arch. It alone contains the signature of God, the Creator.

6. The Bible nowhere represents the Sabbath as a ceremonial institution. It has nothing in common with those festival days, which, as a part of the ceremonial code, pointed to Christ.

7. Christ and his apostles taught the perpetuity of the law, and always observed the Sabbath.

Such an accumulation of evidence is enough to justify these pages in giving the No-Sabbath theory no further notice. Nevertheless, it is better to examine its leading claims. The following is a representative passage from the Old Testament :[1]

" The Lord our God made a covenant with us in Horeb." " The Lord made not this covenant with our fathers, but with us, even us, who are all of us alive here this day."

The claim is made that the Decalogue was this covenant. We have shown that the covenant was not God's law, but an agreement between Jehovah and his people, by which they were bound to keep that

[1] Deut. v. 2, 3, 15.

law, and he, upon such obedience, to grant to them certain promised blessings. The case is a very plain one, and needs no further remark, in addition to what has been said on pages fifteen and sixteen. The fifteenth verse reads as follows:

"And remember that thou wast a servant in the land of Egypt, and that the Lord thy God brought thee out thence through a mighty hand and by a stretched-out arm; therefore the Lord thy God commanded thee to keep the Sabbath day."

In the face of the plain statement made by Jehovah in the Decalogue, the claim is here made that the deliverance from Egypt was the cause why the Sabbath was instituted. The reader will remember that the goodness of God in delivering the Israelites from bondage is often used as a reason for their obedience to all his commandments.[1] If, therefore, the claim of the No-Sabbath theory be correct, *all* the laws of the Decalogue were given for that reason. This is absurd. The whole truth is contained in a single sentence, namely: God's goodness to the Israelites is presented as a reason why *they should obey him.* In the case quoted, the latter clause of the fourteenth verse shows that the Israelites were there urged to allow their servants the blessing of the Sabbath rest, and they are referred to their own bondage in Egypt

[1] See Exodus. xx. 2. Lev. xxvi. 13. Ps. lxxxi. 9, 10, etc.

in contrast with their delivered state, to strengthen this appeal. But if there were any doubt as to the correctness of this simple explanation, the fact that the Jews never understood the Sabbath as commemorative of their deliverance from Egypt settles the question. More than this, the "passover" was given and is yet observed, to commemorate that deliverance. Its whole meaning and language befit such an end, while the *rest* of the Sabbath is in no way significant of the *turmoil* and *hurry* of the exode. Besides all this, the No-Sabbath theory contradicts God's plain words, in Genesis, ii. 3; and Exodus, xx. 11.

NO-SABBATHISM IN THE NEW TESTAMENT.

Only a few "proof texts" are quoted from the New Testament in support of the No-Sabbath theory. The following from Paul's letter to the *Romans*[1] is deemed a strong one.

"Him that is weak in the faith receive ye, *but* not to doubtful disputations."[2]

"For one believeth he may eat all things; another who is weak, eateth herbs."

"Let not him that eateth, despise him that eateth not; and let not him which eateth not, judge him that eateth; for God hath received him."

[1] xiv. 1-7.　　[2] "Not to judge his doubtful thoughts."

"Who art thou that judgest another man's servant? To his own master he standeth or falleth; yea he shall be holden up; for God is able to make him stand."

"One man esteemeth one day above another; another esteemeth every day *alike*. Let every man be fully persuaded in his own mind."

"He that regardeth the day, regardeth *it* unto the Lord: and he that regardeth not the day, to the Lord he doth not regard *it*. He that eateth, eateth to the Lord, for he giveth God thanks; and he that eateth not, to the Lord he eateth not, and giveth God thanks."

This passage concerning the observance of days is thus given with its contexts, that the reader may the more readily see what theme Paul is considering. This fourteenth chapter directs how those shall be treated who still cling to that part of the ceremonial code which refers to clean and unclean foods, and certain days which were associated with them. There is no description of the days, or the manner in which they were observed, but every law of just interpretation classifies them with the other ceremonial observances mentioned. It is well known that public and private voluntary fasts abounded among the Jews at this time, in addition to the older ceremonial feasts. Whatever did not touch the question of seeking forgiveness through Christ is thus spoken of as not important enough to be a bar to fellowship, or a source of contention. A similar instance occurs in Gal. iv. 10, where the ceremonial times are grouped as " days, months, times, and years"; in this case, as with those addressed in Hebrews, the tendency seems to have been toward apostasy from Christ by substituting these ceremonial observances for faith. The observance of the Sabbath had never been a part of the ceremonial system. It had always been a prominent feature of the Decalogue, and its observance could not conflict with faith in Christ any more than the observance of the remaining ten commandments could. As a matter of fact, it was reliance on the ceremonial system for purification from sin, rather than on faith in Christ, which the apostle is everywhere opposing. Paul being his own interpreter, makes this doubly sure; for in the *seventh* chapter[1] of this same epistle—Rom.—he speaks of the Decalogue, of which the Sabbath law is a part, in these words:

"Wherefore the law is holy, and the commandment holy, and just, and good."

A careful study of this seventh chapter of Romans will show that Paul places the highest importance upon the observance of that law which convicts of sin, and is thus our "school-master," leading us to

[1] 12th verse.

Christ for forgiveness. And James, speaking of the same law, says:[1]

"For whosoever shall keep the whole law, and yet offend in one *point*, he is guilty of all."

Paul could not say in one breath that such a law was of great importance, and in the next that it was of little or no importance.

The second chapter of Colossians[2] is often quoted as a clear statement of the No-Sabbath theory.

"Let no man therefore judge you in meat or in drink,[3] or in respect of an holy day,[4] or of the new moon, or of the sabbath *days*;"[5]

"Which are a shadow of things to come; but the body is Christ."

Here it is claimed that the "sabbaths" are distinctly included among things indifferent. Note, first, it is not said that they are abrogated; the most that can be made of the expression is that they are not to be made a matter of dissension or condemnation. Looking at the passage more closely we find that four of the things mentioned are certainly ceremonial: eating, drinking, feasts and new moons.

[1] ii. 10.
[2] 16th and 17th verses.
[3] Greek, "for eating or drinking."
[4] Greek, "concerning the participating in a holy festival."
[5] Greek, "Sabbaths."

The fifth item, "sabbaths," is in the same construction, and stands in the midst of the sentence. If the expression does include the weekly Sabbath, it is an illogical and unwarrantable effort to take an eternal law from the heart of the Decalogue, and class it with temporary ceremonial precepts, for the sake of abrogating it. Christ never ventured such an attack on the law of God, as Paul makes here, if he means the weekly Sabbath. But we are not left in doubt as to what "sabbaths" are meant, for, without stopping to take breath, Paul defines them as being, like the other items, shadows, types of Christ. Whatever the word "sabbaths" might mean considered alone, the definition given here cannot include the weekly Sabbath. That antedated the ceremonial code many centuries. The law of the fourth commandment was placed in the heart of the Decalogue, before the ceremonial code was compiled. God knew where it belonged. The reason given for enacting the fourth commandment is perfectly plain. It was a memorial of God as Creator. It is never spoken of as a type of Christ. The Jews never understood it to be such. If the fourth commandment was a type of Christ, and is done away, then each of its nine associates is in the same category. Even the obscure passage in the 4th of Hebrews makes it a type of heaven, if a type at all. The construction of the passage in Colossians, and the definition given, both preclude the idea that the weekly Sabbath is meant.

The third chapter of second Corinthians is also impressed to do duty in defense of the No-Sabbath theory. The following passage embodies the testimony, so-called:

"But if the ministration of death written *and* engraven in stones was glorious, so that the children of Israel could not steadfastly look upon the face of Moses for the glory of his countenance—which *glory* was to be done away—how shall not the ministration of the spirit be rather glorious?" etc.[1]

A careful reading will show that the contrast here introduced is between the glory of the Mosaic dispensation as compared with the Gospel. It is not the Decalogue which is to be "done away," but the "glory" of the former ministration, which must be lost before the surpassing glory of the later one. Read again the passage and its contexts.

These passages form the stronghold of the No-Sabbath theory in the New Testament. We leave them without further remark, pausing to call the attention of the reader to the utter ruin which this theory works in the realm of moral obligation:

[1] 7th and 8th verses.

1. If the Decalogue was abolished by the death of Christ, then Christ by his death prevented the possibility of sin, to redeem man from which, he died.

2. "Sin is not imputed where there is no law,[1] hence the consciousness of sin which men feel under the claims of the gospel is a mockery, and all faith in Christ is but a farce. It only increases the difficulty to say that the law is written in the hearts of believers. If that be true, then:

3. None but believers in Christ can be convicted of sin, for no others can know the law which convicts of sin. Therefore those who reject Christ, thereby become, at least negatively, *righteous* by refusing to come where they can be convicted of sin. Thus does the No-Sabbath theory make infidelity better than belief, and *rejection of Christ the only means of salvation*. It leads to endless absurdities, and the overthrow of all moral government. It contradicts the plain words of God, and puts darkness for light. Its fruitage in human life has been only bitterness and ashes.

[1] Rom. v. 13.

CHAPTER V.

CHANGE OF THE DAY THEORY.

The Puritan branch of Protestants claims that the Sabbath has been changed, by divine authority, from the seventh to the first day of the week. This theory is based upon the assumption that the Sabbath institution is a separate thing from the Sabbath day, and hence that the Sabbath law may be applied to any seventh portion of time. In opposition to this theory it has been shown:

1. That the Sabbath law and the Sabbath day are inseparable, and that the Sabbatic institution is the result of obedience to the Sabbath law, and ceases to exist when that law is broken.

2. That there could have been no Sabbath if God had not rested on a definite day, for a definite purpose, which no other day could answer. Having rested on a definite day, he blessed and sanctified a definite day, and thus made it *the* Sabbath. To say that the Sabbath is only an indefinite seventh part of time, is to say that God rested on an indefinite seventh part of

time, and blessed an indefinite seventh part of time, all of which is illogical and unscriptural. This theory also "begs the question" by adhering to the septenary division of time, and rejecting the definite day. Upon such an illogical assumption the whole theory of a change of the Sabbath is based. Nevertheless we shall examine the reasons offered in its support in detail. They are as follows:

1. Christ rose from the dead on the first day of the week.

2. The apostles met on that day for public worship, and to commemorate his resurrection.

The first reason is usually separated into the following propositions:

(*a*) Redemption is a greater work than creation.

(*b*) Redemption was completed at the resurrection of Christ.

(*c*) Christ rose from the dead on the first day of the week.

Conclusion. Therefore, since the resurrection, the Sabbath law applies to the first day of the week, and not to the seventh.

It were answer enough to the above theory to suggest that the conclusion is not a legitimate deduction from the premises. Indeed, the premises overthrow the conclusion; for, if "redemption" is a greater work than "creation" and different, then that which was only sufficient to commemorate creation cannot commemorate redemption. Different works must be differently commemorated, and the *greater* cannot be commemorated by that which only measures the *less*. Again, the seventh day can only cease to be sacred, and hence to be the Sabbath, when the causes which make it the Sabbath shall cease to exist. This can never be, since those causes were the words and acts of the infinite Jehovah.

These propositions are equally unsound when considered separately. The first one, in saying that "Redemption is a greater work than creation," assumes that finite man can measure the work of "Creation," and comprehend the goodness, power and wisdom of the Infinite One as therein displayed; that he can look into and understand the work of Redemption as the angels desired to do, but were not able; can comprehend the infinite love and mercy of God as wrought out in that plan, and having thus comprehended and measured two infinite works, can compare one with the other, and decide which of them *is the greater infinity*. Such presumption and want of logic combine to crush the proposition which contains them.

The second proposition asserts that "Redemption was completed at the resurrection of Christ." This is faulty in point of fact. The work of redemption began with the advent of sin. Christ was as a lamb slain from the foundation of the world.[1] The first sacrifice that smoked on the altars of Eden told of redemption. The work of the Redeemer will continue until, as Judge of men, he shall put all things under his feet, and deliver up the kingdom unto his Father. Instead of ceasing the work at his resurrection, Christ ascended to the right hand of the Father, to be our intercessor, until, in the fullness of time, he shall deliver the redeemed and glorified universe up to God.[2] If any one point marks the close of the earth-life of Christ as Redeemer among men, it is the hour of his death, when he cried, "it is finished," and died.[3] Hence the second proposition fails.

The third proposition—"Christ rose from the grave on the first day of the week"—has been accepted without question by the majority of those who will read these pages. Neither the fact of the resurrection, nor the time when it occurred, has any logical connection with the Sabbath question, or rightful place in the Sabbath argument; but since the public mind associates the two questions, it is needful to pass this third proposition under a careful review in order that the reader may see on what sandy grounds the popular theory rests.

[1] Rev. xiii. 8.   [2] 1 Corinthians xv. 24—29.   [3] John xix. 30.

TIME OF CHRIST'S RESURRECTION.

Before taking up the historic accounts of the resurrection by the evangelists, certain outlying facts need to be examined. Christ uttered an important prophecy concerning this matter in the *twelfth* chapter of Matthew,[1] which reads as follows:

"Then certain of the Scribes and Pharisees answered him, saying; Master, we would see a sign from thee."

"But he answered and said unto them, an evil and adulterous generation seeketh after a sign, and there shall no sign be given to it, but the sign of Jonah the prophet."

"For as Jonah was three days and three nights in the belly of the whale: so shall the Son of man be three days and three nights in the heart of the earth."

The circumstances forbid all indefiniteness of expression. It is a case in which Christ offers to his enemies a test involving not simply the truthfulness of his words, but the proof that he was the Son of God. In keeping with this thought, the language respecting the time is carefully and exactly worded.

The Greek says:

Ὥσπερ γὰρ ἦν Ἰωνᾶς ἐν τῇ κοιλίᾳ τοῦ κήτους τρεῖς ἡμέρας καὶ τρεῖς νύκτας, οὕτως ἔσται ὁ υἱός τοῦ ἀνθρώπου ἐν τῇ καρδίᾳ τῆς γῆς τρεῖς ἡμέρας καὶ τρεῖς νύκτας.

The Latin says:

---

[1] 38—41st verses.

TIME OF CHRIST'S RESURRECTION. 51

"Sicut enim fuit Jonas in ventre ceti tres dies et tres noctes: sic erit Fillius hominis in corde terrae tres dies et tres noctes."

The original account in Jonah[1] reads as follows:

"And Jonah was in the belly of the fish three days and three nights."

The Greek of the Septuagint, says:

Καὶ ἦν Ἰωνᾶς ἐν τῇ κοιλίᾳ τοῦ κήτους τρεῖς ἡμέρας καὶ τρεῖς νύκτας.

The Hebrew is in the same construction and equally definite. It is omitted for want of Hebrew type.

In this prophecy one point is unmistakably established, namely: the length of the time during which Christ must remain in the grave. This forms the basis for investigation.

The time when Christ was entombed is equally clear and definite. Matthew[2] says:

"And when even was come, there came a rich man from Arimathea named Joseph, who also himself was Jesus' disciple."

"This man went to Pilate and asked for the body of Jesus. Then Pilate commanded it to be given up.

"And Joseph took the body, and wrapped it in a clean linen cloth, and laid it in his own new tomb which he had hewn out in the rock; and he rolled a great stone to the door of the tomb and departed."

The Greek of the passage which refers to the

[1] i. 17. [2] xxvii. 57—61.

time, is: 'Οψιάς δὲ γενομένης, literally, "when it was late." John corroborates the words of Matthew and shows[1] that it was late in the day, just before the setting of the sun, that the body of Christ was laid in the grave. By the words of his own prophecy, then, he must have risen at an hour in the day corresponding to the hour of his entombment. Thus two points are established, namely: the time of the day when the resurrection must occur, *late in the day*, and the length of time which must intervene between the entombment and the resurrection, three days and three nights. We are now prepared to examine the history of the resurrection as given by the evangelists.

Three of the evangelists speak of the resurrection only in general terms, giving neither the time when it occurred, nor the circumstances attending it. John says:[2]

"Now on the first *day* of the week cometh Mary Magdalene early, while it was yet dark, unto the tomb, and seeth the stone taken away from the tomb," etc.

Luke says:[3]

"But on the first *day* of the week, at early dawn, they came unto the tomb, bringing the spices which they had prepared."

[1] xix. 31, 38, 42.
[2] xx. 1.
[3] xxiv. 1—3

"And they found the stone rolled away from the tomb."

"And they entered in, and found not the body of the Lord Jesus."

Mark says :[1]

"And when the Sabbath was past, Mary Magdalene and Mary the *Mother* of James, and Salome, bought spices, that they might come and annoint him."

"And very early on the first *day* of the week, they come to the tomb when the sun was risen."

These accounts teach nothing more than the fact that when the parties mentioned visited the sepulchre, they found it empty. Christ had risen and gone. But Matthew gives an account quite different, and more definite; one which tells of a visit *previous* to the one spoken of by the other three writers just examined. The following is the account :[2]

Now late on the Sabbath-day, as it began to dawn toward the first *day* of the week came Mary Magdalene, and the other Mary to see the sepulchre."

"And behold there was[3] a great earthquake; for an angel of the Lord descended from heaven, and came and rolled away the stone, and sat upon it."

"His appearance was as lightning and his raiment white as snow."

"And for fear of him the watchers did quake, and became as dead *men*."

[1] xvi. 2.
[2] xxviii. 1-8.
[3] Margin. "had been"; Greek, ἐγένετο

"And the angel answered and said unto the women, Fear not ye; for I know that ye seek Jesus which hath been crucified."

"He is not here; for he is risen even as he said, come, see the place where the Lord lay;" etc.

Here is an account minute in details respecting both the time of the resurrection, and the circumstances connected with it. It agrees in all particulars with the requirements of the prophecy of Christ and the time of his entombment. The opening clause of the twenty-eighth chapter fixes the time, "Late in the Sabbath."[1] *The Sabbath closed at sunset.*

This point of time exactly corresponds to the hour of the entombment. No amount of "surmising" or "supposing" can change this plain statement. If the exegetical argument be sought from the construction of the Greek it is equally as plain and strong. The possessive idea denoted by the genitive necessitates that the point of time denoted by ὀψέ be contained *within* the time denoted by the noun. So here, σαββάτων holds ὀψέ within its limits. Ὀψέ, when constructed with a verb in the infinitive may sometimes mean "after," in the sense of "too late," when referring to an action. But in the case under consideration it can not thus mean. No commentator has attempted to thus interpret this

[1] Ὀψέ δὲ σαββάτων.

passage except upon the assumption or upon the *supposition* that Matthew meant something which he did not say, and that his account must be *forced* to agree with the other three, and thus give some shadow of support to an inferential "harmony." Nor is the word translated "dawn" opposed to the view here expressed. It is ἐπιφωσκούσῃ from Ἐπιφώσκω. This is used but once, besides this, in the New Testament. That use is by Luke,[1] where the Passover Sabbath following the crucifixion is said to "draw on." Here the term is used concerning the day closing at sunset. This is a natural and legitimate translation of the word, and there is no reason why it should not be thus rendered in Matthew xxviii. 1. Such a rendering only, agrees with the facts. The Sabbath closed at sunset on the seventh day of the week. At the same hour the first day of the week "drew on," "came in sight," "began to appear." Translators of the New Testament have been more truthful to the correct rendering than interpreters have been to the correct exegesis, as the following facts testify:

The Syriac Peshito version, renders this passage, "In the evening of the Sabbath." The Latin of the Vulgate renders it by the same words. Beza's Latin

[1] xxiii. 54.

translation has the same. Tyndale's translation says: "The Sabbath-day at even." Coverdale's translation reads. "Upon the evening of the Sabbath holy day." Cranmer's, the Genevan, and the Bishop's versions, all render it, "In the latter end of the Sabbath-day." The Greek is literally—"Late in the Sabbath." Rotherham's Critically Emphasized Version, says: "And late in [the] week, when it was on the point of dawning into [the] the first of [the] week," etc. Alford—Greek Gospels—acknowledges the important fact, but attempts to make Matthew accord with the other evangelists by "supposing" that he meant something different from what he says. These are Alford's words.

"There is some little difficulty here, because the end of the Sabbath (and of the week) *was at sunset the night before*. It is hardly to be supposed that Matthew means the *evening* of the Sabbath, though ἐπέφωσκε is used of the day beginning at sunset.[1] It is best to interpret a doubtful expression in unison with other testimonies, and to suppose that here both the *day* and the *breaking of the day*, are taken in their *natural*, not in their *Jewish* sense.

On Luke xxiii. 54, Alford says:[2]

"ἐπέφωσκεν, '*drew on*,' a *natural* word, used of the *conventional* (Jewish) day beginning at sunset. There is no reference to the lighting of candles in the evening, or

---

[1] Luke xxiii. 54, and note.
[2] *Greek Gospels.*

on the Sabbath. Lightfoot (in loc.) has shown that such a use of the word was common among the Jews who called the evening (the beginning) of a day, 'light.' "

The italics in the above are Alford's. His scholarship is far better than his effort to make Matthew's account harmonize with the rest of the Evangelists. His words as a scholar, forbid his *supposition* as a theologian. There is nothing "doubtful" in the meaning of Matt. xxviii. 1, when it is allowed to say what it does say.

About 1865, the writer published the proposition that Christ's entombment occurred on the evening of the fourth day of the week, and his resurrection before the close of the Sabbath, and not upon the first day of the week. The proposition was met with a storm of criticism by some, and with careful consideration by others. This interpretation has gained ground steadily, until the highest authorities in New Testament criticism now support it. The revisers of the New Testament have given it absolute sanction, by translating as above. To place the matter still farther beyond dispute there has lately appeared a "*Greek-English Lexicon of the New Testament, Grimm's Wilke's Clavis Novi Testamenti*. Translated, Revised and Enlarged, by Joseph Henry Thayer, D. D., Bussey Professor of New Testament Criticism and

Interpretation in the Divinity School of Harvard University": in which the construction of Matthew xxviii. 1 is fully discussed. After giving the references which have been adduced in support of the translation "after the Sabbath," Prof. Thayer says:

"But an examination of the instances just cited (and others) will show that they fail to sustain the rendering *after* (although it is recognized by Passow, Pape, Schenkel and other lexicographers) : ὀψέ, followed by a genitive, seems always to be *partitive*, denoting *late in* the period specified by the genitive, (and consequently still belonging to it,) cf. B. sec. 132, 7 Rem. Kuehner sec. 414, 5 c. β. Hence in Matthew [l. c.] *late* on the Sabbath. Keim. iii. p. 552, seq. [Eng. trans. vi. 303, seq.] endeavors to relieve the passage differently (by adopting the *Vulg.*, *vespere Sabbati:* on the evening of the Sabbath), but without success. Compare Keil, Com. ueber Matt. *Ad loc.*"

Thus is the weight of past and present scholarship thrown in favor of the explanation here given. This explanation shows that the prophecy of Christ, and the accounts of the entombment, and of the resurrection agree with extreme fidelity. And the accounts of the Evangelists agree with each other when the fact is thus recognized that, in the opening of the twenty-eighth chapter, Matthew speaks of the *first* visit to the sepulchre "late in the Sabbath," to which visit the other evangelists do not refer; they describe a *second* visit made early on the following morning. Matthew's account of the first visit evidently closes with the eighth verse, and in the ninth he passes to the scenes of the next morning. Thus the following conclusions are fixed.

Christ was crucified and entombed on the fourth day of the week, commonly called Wednesday. He lay in the grave " three days and three nights" and rose " late in the Sabbath," at an hour corresponding with the hour of his entombment, at which time two of the women came to see the sepulchre.

There is certain circumstantial evidence which corroborates these conclusions:

1. Since Christ gave the length of time he should lie in the grave as a sign of his Messiahship, any failure in the fulfillment of that sign would have been noted and published by his enemies. The fact that no such charge has ever been made, and only the puerile story of the stealing of the body invented, is evidence that the prophecy was exactly fulfilled.

2. On the day following the crucifixion the Jews went to Pilate, sought a guard for the tomb for three days, and attended to the setting of it. This they would not have done on the weekly Sabbath; but they would not shrink from doing it on the Passover Sabbath which they observed less strictly.

3. The guard was set to cover a time three days from the entombment. Until that time expired not even the disciples, much less two lone women, would attempt to reach the tomb to look after the body. Hence the women spoken of in Matthew *twenty-eighth*, came to the tomb with the evident design of being present the moment the guard should be removed.

On the other hand if the popular theory be correct, Christ was laid in the grave late on the sixth day of the week, the guard was set on the seventh day, and on that same day, scarcely twenty-four hours after the entombment the women are found at the sepulchre, and Christ is risen. Such conclusions contradict the plain statements of the Word, and are out of accord with all the circumstances in the case. A circumstantial "objection" to the explanation here given is made on the claim that the two women would not be likely to make a second visit to the sepulchre on the following morning. The reverse is the most natural conclusion. A second visit was necessary to confirm the hopes which the strange scenes of the previous evening had awakened. Hence their eagerness; and taking other witnesses, they hasten "while it was yet dark" to come again to the sacred spot to see if indeed their Lord had risen. This is farther confirmed by the fact already indicated, that the eighth verse of Matthew twenty-eighth seems to close the account of the first visit; while from the ninth verse to the close of the chapter we have in four separate paragraphs, the whole history of the circumstances of the next morning and of the entire time up to the Ascension of Christ, crowded into eleven verses.

An indirect objection to this view of the time of the resurrection is based on the scenes connected with Christ's appearance to the two disciples, on the way to Emmaus, on the day after his resurrection. It is claimed that Luke xxiv. 21, indicates the burial on Friday and the resurrection on Sunday. Examining this chapter we find,[1] that they were talking of "*All these things which had happened.*" In the 21st verse, the disciples answer Christ:

"Yea, and beside all this, it is now the third day *since* these things came to pass."

Now it is very clear that conversation concerning the reported resurrection must have included a discussion of the important fact that after all else had occurred, and Christ was buried, a guard had been set to prevent his resurrection. That was the last act in the scenes of his death and burial. If the language of the two disciples in Luke xxiv. 21, be

[1] 14th verse.

taken absolutely, then according to the explanation we have given of the time of the entombment and the setting of the guard, Friday would have been the first day "since" the placing of the guard, for the guard was set on *Thursday*, and Sunday would have been the third day *since* all these things happened. On the other hand, if the Romish tradition of the burial on Friday, and the placing of the guard on the Sabbath, be accepted, there is no possibility of making Sunday more than the *first day* "since" these things were done.

The obvious meaning of Luke xxiv. 21, is this. "The time is now fully up *since* the final effort was made to prevent a resurrection, and this morning the women reported that in spite of all efforts to the contrary, it had actually taken place." Nevertheless we are willing, so far as the argument is concerned, that the language should be interpreted with the most absolute exactness; which being done, our explanation of the time of the entombment and of the resurrection is the only one with which it can be made to accord.

It is now pertinent to group together these objections to the popular notion concerning the resurrection.

1. There is nowhere in the Bible any statement that Christ rose on the first day of the week.

TIME OF CHRIST'S RESURRECTION. 63

2. The popular claim contradicts the plain words of Matthew who alone gives the time when the resurrection occurred.

3. The claim that Christ was entombed late on the sixth day of the week disagrees entirely with the express conditions laid down by Christ in his prophetic words concerning the time he should lie in the grave; therefore:

4. If the popular theory be corrrct, Christ's prophecy was not fulfilled, and, by his own words, he is proven to have been an impostor. The circumstances connected with the burial and resurrection must also be tortured into unnatural relations and forced harmony. We can therefore only repeat the conclusion that Christ *did not rise on the first day of the week*. Thus, step by step, the assumptions in favor of a change of the Sabbath, based upon the resurrection of Christ, are swept away.

CHAPTER VI.

CHRIST'S EXAMPLE CONCERNING THE FIRST DAY OF THE WEEK.

The remaining effort at argument in favor of the change, is predicated upon the claim that Christ and his apostles authorized a change of the day, by their example in observing the first day of the week. It is hence necessary to examine the passages which are quoted in favor of such observance, in their order, and with their contexts.

The first passage is found in John xx. 19—23. All our readers have the "common version" and many of them have others, and the original from which to make their own. To aid in a better understanding of the text we present the Revised Version, the corrected translation as given in Lange's Commentary, and also the "Critically Emphasized Translation" of Joseph B. Rotherham. (Bagster, London, 1878.) These are as follows:

" When therefore it was evening, on that day, the first *day* of the week, and when the doors were shut where the disciples were, for fear of the Jews, Jesus came and stood in the midst, and saith unto them, peace *be* unto you. And when he had said this, he showed unto them his hands and his side. The disciples therefore were glad, when they saw the Lord. Jesus therefore said to them again, peace *be* unto you: as the Father hath sent me, even so send I you. And when he had said this, he breathed on them, and saith unto them, Receive ye the Holy Ghost; whosoever sins ye forgive, they are forgiven unto them; whosoever *sins* ye retain, they are retained."[1]

"When, therefore, it was evening on that day, the first of the week, and the doors had been shut, or, the doors being shut, where the disciples were for fear of the Jews, came Jesus and stood in the midst, and saith unto them, Peace *be* unto you. And having said this, he showed unto them both his hands and his side. The disciples therefore were glad when they saw the Lord. Then he said to them again, Peace *be* unto you. As the Father hath sent me, even so send I you. And when he had said this, he breathed on *them*, and saith unto them, Receive Holy Spirit. Whosoever sins ye remit, they have been remitted; and whosoever ye retain, they have been retained."[2]

In the following, the italic type indicates the Greek emphasis, and not "supplied words," as in the ordinary version; the brackets denote supplied words:

"It being late, therefore, on that day—the first of [the] week—and the doors having been fastened where

[1] Revised Version. [2] Lange.

the disciples were, by reason of the fear of the Jews, Jesus came and stood in the midst, and says to them, Peace to you! and this saying, he pointed out both [his] hands and [his] side to them. The disciples, therefore, *rejoiced*, seeing the Lord! He said to them again, therefore, Peace to you! According as the *Father* has sent *me* forth, I also send *you*. And this saying he breathed strongly, and says to them, Receive ye Holy Spirit! Whosesoever sins ye may remit, they have been remitted unto them: whosesoever ye may be retaining, they have been retained."[1]

Such is the brief history of the appearing of Christ to his disciples on the evening after the day on which his resurrection had become known. It is claimed that this was a meeting of the disciples to commemorate, sabbatically, the resurrection. Observe, first that no such thing is either said or implied in the text. On the contrary, it is distinctly stated that they were secreted, with fastened doors, "for fear of the Jews." But let us look more fully into the doings of that day. From Luke (24th chapter) we have seen that when the women told the circumstances of the morning to the eleven disciples "their words seemed as idle tales, and they believed them not."

In the same chapter it is related that two of the disciples journeyed to Emmaus, seven and one-half

[1] Rotherham.

miles, during that day. Christ joined them on the journey, and at supper revealed himself to them. They, wondering and rejoicing, returned to Jerusalem. While they related their story to the other disciples, Christ came. Even then they would not believe until he explained his former words concerning himself. Thus it is clear that they did not believe in his resurrection until late in the evening. They could not have been together to celebrate an event *in which they did not believe*. It was to cure this unbelief, to *prove* his resurrection and not to celebrate it, that Christ came. The hatred which raged against the disciples necessitated that they should secrete themselves from the fury of the Jews. On the evening in question they were thus hidden away, in despondency, sorrow, and doubt. Had this been a meeting held for the purpose of instituting so radical a change in a practice so widely affecting Christian life, and based upon a fact not until then believed, it is impossible to suppose that no mention would be made of the fact by the risen Saviour who alone had power to make a change if one were possible. His silence disproves the claim. It is an important fact also that the best commentators, like Alford, Meyer, Schaff, Lange, and Ellicott, make no effort to draw from this passage any support whatever for Sunday observance. It is only when men are anxious to find a Scriptural warrant for observing Sunday, that, as polemists, and not as commentators, they attempt to put into this record what neither Christ nor the Holy Spirit, guiding John, put into it. Whoever attempts to make the passage support Sunday-keeping, has to assume that the Spirit left the account imperfect, and that men have a right to complete it by reading "between the lines," what is not written. This passage has a still more important bearing on the whole question, since this first meeting for the purpose of proving his resurrection was the natural and obvious time for him to add, "And henceforth you are to observe the day just passed, in honor of my resurrection, as the Sabbath in place of the day before, which you and I have hitherto observed." Such words from Christ would have put the question at rest. That he said nothing of the kind is proof that he meant nothing of the kind. And more: No writer in the New Testament refers to this meeting as the beginning of Sunday observance, or as authority for it. The whole claim was an afterthought, comparatively modern, to support a practice, introduced for other reasons.

The second passage which is claimed in support of Sunday observance, is from the same chapter, John

(xx. 26). It is as follows, and is more indefinite than the one just considered:

"And after eight days, again his disciples were within, and Thomas with them. Jesus cometh, the doors being shut, and stood in the midst, and said, Peace be unto you."

It is claimed that this was the next first day, on the ground that "Sunday and Sunday make eight," and that the meeting was again in honor of the resurrection. But the account does not state that it was upon the eighth day, but "after eight days." Now the English *after*, the Latin *post*, and the Greek *meta*, are among the most positive words in these languages; and if the time spoken of was exact, it must have been upon the ninth day at least. If the expression is indefinite, in the sense of the English expression "about eight days after," then the case is so much the worse for the argument. Admitting that it was the next first day, there is no implication of any sabbatic character connected with the meeting. The simple fact of the case being this: Thomas being absent from the former meeting would not believe that Christ had risen. At this time Thomas is present, and is convinced. The fact that Christ instructed them, proves nothing sabbatic, or celebrative, for his next meeting (see next chapter,) was upon a day when they were fishing, when he instructed them more fully than at any time before.

These two passages constitute the entire array of proof, so called, that Christ honored the first day of the week, or taught its observance. And yet many polemists, writing in favor of the change of the Sabbath, refer to these passages as though they were two among many which might be quoted if necessary. If Christ taught the observance of Sunday, or the change of the Sabbath, we are anxious to know it, and to act accordingly. But something more than these two passages, and the inferences which are put into them—not *drawn from* them—is necessary to form any foundation for setting aside a plain command of the Decalogue.

TESTIMONY FROM THE BOOK OF ACTS.

The first day of the week is mentioned but once in the book of Acts. Nevertheless two passages are cited from the book, in support of Sunday observance. The first is as follows:

"And when the day of Pentecost was now come, they were all together in one place." Acts ii. 1.

Surely no one seeking proof for the change of the Sabbath from apostolic example, would think of finding it in this text. Nothing appears in the text or the contexts to indicate on what day of the week the occurrences described, happened, or to show that the passsage has the remotest connection with the Sabbath question. Something must be read into the text, in order to make any mention of the question before us. How is this done? After this manner: "The Pentecost fell on the first day of the week; God poured out his spirit miraculously on that day, thus sanctifying it, or, at least showing it an especial favor." Let us see whether the major premise of this proposition is true, viz.: that the Pentecost fell on First day. It was a yearly feast, falling on the fiftieth day reckoning from the day following the Passover. Thus reckoning, this Pentecost would have fallen on the first day of the week *if* the Saviour had been crucified on the sixth day, and the Passover been held, as is claimed, on the seventh. We have already shown that such was *not* the case; hence the premise is incorrect in point of fact.

We are by no means alone in claiming that this Pentecost did not fall on Sunday. No one can conclude that it did fall on Sunday except by *assuming* that Christ was crucified on Friday, and that that Friday was the fourteenth day of the month Nisan. This is a disputed point. Dr. Schaff acknowledges that with reference to the question whether this Pentecost fell on the Sabbath or on the Sunday, "Opinions are much divided, and the arguments almost equally balanced." Any one reading the opinions of the various writers concerning the day of Christ's death, and the consequent day of the Pentecost referred to in Acts second, will see how hopeless is the confusion to which men rush who are obliged to *assume* important points. The explanation which we have given of the time of the resurrection, and the length of time Christ should lie in the grave, both of which are fixed by Matthew (xxviii. 1, and xii. 40), makes complete harmony between Christ's prophetic words, and their fulfilment. It also gives a complete "Harmony of the Gospels," without assuming anything which is not absolutely stated in the Gospels, except that there were two visits to the sepulchre. The traditions and customs of the early church which were developed in post-apostolic times, are of no value, if they do not agree with the inspired Records. Hence we conclude that the Pentecost of Acts ii. 1, did not fall upon the first day of the week. But had it fallen upon the first day, there was nothing in this demonstration of God's spirit which had reference to the day of the week. It was the Pentecost which they met to celebrate, and while thus celebrating, the miraculous out pouring came. The reason for choosing the Pentecost as the time at which to manifest thus the power of the Spirit is evident in the fact that thousands of devout men from every land were there, and being convinced of the truth of Christianity, would carry that truth far and wide as they returned home. There is another significant fact which alone overthrows the popular claim. The writer of the passage says nothing concerning the day of the week. Had it been the first day, just adopted by the apostles as the Christian Sabbath, it is not conceivable that so marked an occurrence in its favor would have been passed in utter silence. This closes the proof (?) which is offered to show that Christ by example or precept, or the Holy Spirit by special sanction, taught or in any way authorized the change of the Sabbath.

CHAPTER VII.

EXAMPLE OF THE APOSTLES.

The history of the doings and teachings of the apostles is equally devoid of any proof in favor of the popular theory. The book of Acts covers at least thirty years of time after the resurrection of Christ. This is the period during which it is claimed that the change was going on under the direction of the Apostles and the Holy Spirit. Two stubborn facts oppose this claim.

1. The resurrection of Christ as the proof of his Messiahship, is a prominent theme in the sermons which the apostles preached during this period. This was especially dwelt upon in the sermon of Peter at Pentecost, and many times thereafter.

Such preaching could not avoid the discussion of the change of the Sabbath, as based upon the resurrection, if the change had been then going on. This fact is the more significant since Luke, the writer of the book of Acts, is especially careful to notice any compliance with existing customs. Notice the following passages from his Gospel:

"According to the custom of the priest's office, his lot was to enter into the temple of the Lord and burn incense."[1] "And when the parents brought in the child Jesus that they might do concerning him after the custom of the law."[2] "And he came to Nazareth, where he had been brought up, and he entered, as his custom was, into the synagogue on the Sabbath-day."[3] "And he came out and went, as his custom was, unto the Mount of Olives."[4]

In the book of Acts, he says:

"And on the Sabbath-day, we went forth without the gate by a river side, where we supposed there was a place of prayer."[5] "They came to Thessalonica, where was a synagogue of the Jews; and Paul, as his custom was, went in unto them."[6]

These passages show that it was characteristic of Luke to notice compliance with existing customs, even when no especial interest was attached to the fact. How, then, can we suppose that the establishment of a new custom, so important, and so full of interest to the narrative, could be passed over in silence.

The single passage in which a reference is made to the first day of the week, in the book of Acts, is in the twentieth chapter, and seventh verse. It is as follows:

[1] i. 9.   [2] ii. 27.   [3] iv. 16.
[4] xxii. 39.   [5] xvi. 13.   [6] xvii. 1, 2.

"And upon the first *day* of the week, when we were gathered together to break bread, Paul discoursed with them, intending to depart on the morrow and prolonged his speech until midnight."

It is claimed that this passage indicates a well-understood custom of sabbatizing on the first day of the week. But there are the same difficulties here as in the cases before examined. Luke is a careful writer, and often speaks of established customs. The account in this place is a minute one. In the third verse, and those following it, we are told how Paul dwelt three months in Greece, who accompanied him, and where they were from, who came with him on the voyage toward Troas, certain of whom went before, while Paul and others of the party, Luke included, remained at Philippi until after the days of unleavened bread and then set out for Troas where they arrived after five days' journey and remained seven days. The evening before they set out for Assos, the inhabitants came in; and so follows the minute account of the meeting and its attendant circumstances. Now could a writer so minute in unimportant matters, pass over in silence the fact that they there celebrated the new institution of the resurrection day, had such been the case; especially when the day is mentioned? This is the more wonderful since he nowhere else even mentions the first day of the week in any manner whatever. According to the popular theory, this passage refers only to the evening. If the day was observed by them as a Sabbath there must have been religious services during the day, and these would naturally be more prominent than the evening service; why then should so careful and exact a writer pass over the more important features of the case in silence, and leave the less important features with only a vague reference. Such a claim does great injustice to the scholarship of Luke, saying nothing of his inspiration.

All this is upon the popular supposition that the meeting was held on what is now called Sunday evening, and that the breaking of bread was a "celebration of the Lord's Supper." There are imperative reasons for rejecting both these interpretations. According to the Jewish method of reckoning time, which is everywhere used by the writers of the Bible, all of whom were Jews, this meeting must have been on the evening after the Sabbath, on what is now called "Saturday" evening, and hence Paul and his companions traveled all the next day. If to avoid this dilemma, the Roman reckoning be *supposed*, then the main item of the meeting, viz. : the "Breaking of bread," took place after midnight, and hence on the second day of the week. Either horn of this dilemma destroys whatever of inferential evidence this passage might otherwise be supposed to afford.

The time when this meeting was held is given by Conybear and Howson as follows :

"The labors of the early days of the week that was spent at Troas, are not related to us ; but concerning the last day we have a narrative which enters into details with all the minuteness of one of the gospel histories. It was the evening which succeeded the Jewish Sabbath. On Sunday morning the vessel was about to sail." [1]

The phrase $K\lambda\acute{a}\sigma\alpha\iota\ \acute{a}\rho\tau o\nu$, which is translated, "to break bread" is repeatedly used to designate the eating of a common meal. It is thus used in Acts ii. 46, where the forty-fifth and forty-seventh verses show that these were but ordinary meals. So also in Acts xxvii. 37, the same terms denote the common meal of a company of two hundred and seventy-six. So far as the language or the circumstances decide, it may have been a common meal, or a love feast, or the Lord's Supper. In either case there is nothing in the fact to affect the day. The farewell meeting is sufficient ground for all that occurred, and the

[1] Life and Epistles of St. Paul, chap. xx.

miraculous restoration of the young man, together with the farewell meeting, give abundant reason for placing the incident on record. We have therefore no hesitancy in adopting the conclusion that the meeting spoken of in Acts twentieth and seventh, was an informal gathering of Paul and his traveling companions, with more or less of those who dwelt at Troas, on the evening after the Sabbath. And hence that Paul and his party traveled all day on the following first day of the week.

Ellicott supports this view, in the following words:

"It seems probable that in churches which were so largely organized on the framework of the Jewish synagogue, and contained so many Jews and proselytes who had been familiar with its usages, the Jewish mode of reckoning would still be kept, and that as the Sabbath ended at sunset the first day of the week would begin at sunset on what was then or soon afterwards known as Saturday. In this case the meeting of which we read would be held on what we should call the Saturday evening and the feast would present some analogies to the prevalent Jewish custom of eating bread and drinking wine at that time in honor of the departing Sabbath. '*Ready to depart on the morrow.*' It may perhaps seem strange to some, taking the view maintained in the previous note, that the apostle and his companions should thus purpose to travel on a day to which we have transferred so many of the restrictions of the Jewish Sabbath. But it must be remembered (1) that there is no evidence that St. Paul thought of them as so transferred, but rather the contrary. (Gal. iv. 10. Col. ii. 16.) and (2) that the ship in which his friends had taken their passage was not likely to alter its day of starting to meet their scruples even had these scruples existed."[1]

Dr. Smith speaks of this service as follows, after showing how fully the customs of the earlier churches grew out of the synagogue, both as regards forms and times of service:

"It was a Jewish custom to end the Sabbath with a feast, in which they did honor to it as to a parting king. The feast was held in the synagogue. A cup of wine over which a special blessing had been spoken, was handed around. It is obvious that so long as the apostles and their followers continued to use the Jewish mode of reckoning, *i. e.*, so long as they fraternized with their brethren of the stock of Abraham, this would coincide in point of time with their δειπνον on the *first* day of the week."[2]

In conclusion we ask the reader to contrast this one meagre and indefinite reference to the first day of the week in all the history of the doings of the Apostles for thirty years after Christ, with the repeated recognition of the Sabbath in the book of Acts, and to decide in the light of the inspired Word,

[1] Commentary, vol ii., p. 138.
[2] Bible Dictionary, Art. "Synagogue."

what the example of the Apostles was concerning the Sabbath and the Sunday.

THE EPISTLES.

Turning to the epistles the reader will find the same almost absolute silence concerning the first day of the week. In all the New Testament epistles there is but *one* reference to it, and this does not refer to it as the Sabbath, or as commemorative of the resurrection, or as in any way holy or sacred. Had the change been going on, had the first day been pressed upon the attention of the converts, and demands made for its observance, much instruction would have been requisite to bring them—especially the Hebrews, to obedience. It is against all logic and all experience to think that such a change could have been made during such times, and nothing be said concerning it. Here is the lone passage:

"Now concerning the collection for the Saints, as I gave order to the churches of Galatia, so also do ye. Upon the first day of the week, let each one of you lay by him in store as he may prosper, that no collections be made when I come."[1]

This is claimed by some as an order for a public collection, and hence indicative of a public meeting on that day. The claim is only a far-fetched infer-

[1] 1 Cor. xvi. 1, 2.

ence, and is shown to be unfounded by the expression, "lay by him in store." The text contains no suggestion of a public gathering, but the exact opposite. It is the work of the theologian to put such an interpretation *onto* the passage, and not the work of the scholar to draw it from the passage. In support of this are the following facts:

The English rendering, "let each one of you lay by him in store," clearly indicates a personal work on the part of each man by himself. The Greek is equally plain, and, if possible, stronger. It is as follows:

Κατὰ μίαν σαββάτων ἕκαστος ὑμῶν παρ' ἑαυτῷ τιθέτω, θησαυρίζων ὅ, τι ἂν εὐοδῶται.

It would be difficult to frame a sentence which would express the idea of personal action by one's self, more exactly. It is literally, "each one of you, by himself, lay away, treasuring up." The Latin is:

"Per unam Sabbatorum unusquisque vestrum apud se reponat recondens, quod bene successerit," etc.

Literally, "Each one of you at his own house lay up, putting away," etc.

Tyndale says: "Let every one off you put a syde at home and laye uppe."

The Syriac Peshito, reads as follows: "Let every one of you lay aside and preserve at home."

To this the following may be added:

Three French versions read, "*at his own house at home.*" Luther, "*By himself at home.*" The Dutch version the same. The Italian version, "*In his own presence at home.*" The Spanish, "*In his own house.*" Portuguese, "*With himself.*" Swedish, "*Near himself.*" The Douay Bible, "Let every one of you put apart with himself." Beza, "*At home.*" Rotherham, "*Let each one of you put by itself, treasuring up,*" etc.

Meyer says παρ' ἑαυτῶ τιθέτω cannot refer to the laying down of money in the assembly. His translation is: "*Let him lay up in store at home whatever he succeeds in*, i. e., if he has success in anything, let him lay it up, i. e., *what he has gained thereby*, in order that gatherings be not made when I shall come." (On Cor. vol. ii. p. 111.)

By such an array of scholarship the vague inference on which the common notion rests, is at once destroyed. The direction given by Paul is that each man should begin the work of the week by putting aside as much as he was able, for the poor saints at Jerusalem, in order that each having thus decided what he could do, there need be no delay about the matter when Paul should arrive. This order was only temporary, and for a specific purpose. More than this, it was only five years before that Paul organized the Corinthian church while he was observing the Sabbath. Thus does this passage prove too weak to support even an inference in favor of a change of the Sabbath.

The foregoing conclusion is further supported by the fact that attending to gifts for the poor on the first day of the week was directly in the line of the *customs of the synagogue*. Witness the following:

"The alms for the support of the poor members of the congregation were put into the alms chest before prayers; and on Sabbath evenings what had been collected, was apportioned to the poor for the entire week. Sometimes after the usual collection in the synagogue, there was an extraordinary one made by the Chazzan, for some particular purpose. .... As this was usually done on the Sabbath day (when the Jews do not handle money), each person by word of mouth bound himself to the minister of the synagogue for a certain sum which he paid the following week.

"We may trace the following points of agreement between the church and the synagogue, as to the collection and distribution of alms. In the synagogue alms were collected for a two-fold purpose; for the poor members of the congregation, and for the poor brethren in Judea. The same custom prevailed in the early Christian church. In the synagogue the alms though set apart on the Sabbath were not paid until the first day of the week.

"This superstitious custom of not handling money on the Sabbath is very ancient; thus Philo praises the Emperor Augustus because in his anxiety that the Jews should be partakers of his bounty, he ordered, that if the day of distribution happened to be on the Jewish Sabbath it should be bestowed on the following day."[1]

The above shows that Paul ordered the Corinthians to do what they had been accustomed to do in the case of "special collections," varying his order in only one particular, viz., that instead of paying it into the treasury of the synagogue on the first day of the week, they were to lay it up *at home* until such time as he might arrive.

The attendant circumstances all strengthen the conclusion that this was in keeping with the synagogue practices. Paul wrote this first letter to the Corinthians in the Spring of 57 A. D.[2]

He planted the church at Corinth in 53, A. D.[3]

Like all the earlier churches, it sprang up in and around the synagogue, and among Jews and Jewish Proselytes—Acts xviii. 1-11 ; Paul keeping the Sabbath meanwhile, and in all his stay of eighteen months never uttering a word about the obsoleteness of the Sabbath, or of the new institution of Sunday. Moreover, the advocates of Sunday observance all claim that the change was a matter of slow growth,

---

[1] The Synagogue and the Church, condensed from the Latin of Vitringa, by Joshua L. Bernhard, London, 1842. pp. 76, 166, 175.
[2] Schaff Ch. Hist., Vol. 1, p. 759. Rev. Ed.
[3] Fisher, "Beginnings of Christianity," p. 579.

lest prejudice might be aroused. It is therefore wholly illogical to believe that *within two years and one half* from the time Paul left Corinth after the establishing of the church, so great a change had taken place, so adverse to the practice of the apostle while there, and amid the startling silence which kept Paul from speaking, and Luke from writing any word concerning Sunday. The only natural exegesis of the passage, in the light of the surrounding facts is, that the order to lay aside at home this special contribution, was a slight modification of the ordinary custom, which the circumstances made necessary.

"THE LORD'S DAY."

One more passage remains to complete the survey of proof claimed from the New Testment, Rev. i. 10, " I was in the spirit on the " Lord's day." The claim is made that the "Lord's day" refers to the first day of the week, which presupposes that the day was then observed as a Sabbath, or at least as a day of religious meeting. The only evidence offered, is the presumption that it was thus used then, because it is met with (for the first time) in the writings of one of the Christian Fathers about 170 A. D., and that it afterward came to be used to designate the first day. But the fact that John uses the term nowhere else in all his writings, and that he uses it here in only an incidental manner, and that the writings of the Fathers down to the year 170, of which there are several fragments, make no mention of it, proves conclusively, that in whatever sense John used the term, he did not apply it to the first day of the week. It is also an undisputed fact that when the use of the term became somewhat general, in the third and fourth centuries, no writer attributes its use to the fact that it had been used in the Revelation. This idea is strongly supported by the date of the book, which modern scholarship places at least a quarter of a century *before* the date of John's Gospel.

Accepting this modern date, 68 to 70 A. D. *before* the destruction of Jerusalem,[1] we have more than a quarter of a century elapsing, during which time it is assumed that Sunday observance, as the "Lord's day" was making rapid strides, and yet in his latest writings, John uses only the term first day of the week, for Sunday, and uses that only incidentally in connection with the account of the announcing of the resurrection of Christ. Every law of internal evidence forbids the conclusion that he used the term "Lord's day," as referring to Sunday in the earlier

---

[1] "See Beginnings of Christianity," by Prof. Geo. P. Fisher, p. 534, seq.

writing, and does not use it a quarter of a century later when the term and the day, as is claimed, had grown to be common and universal. The same argument holds good of the Book of Acts, completed 62 or 63 A. D. and including much history which demands some record concerning the day, and the terms by which it was known, if the popular notion be correct, and yet this history mentions the day but once, and that only as the "first day of the week."

Whatever the phrase may mean, there is not in it, or its contexts, evidence that it refers to any day of the week. Like all the rest of the passages referred to in favor of Sunday, it has no point or meaning until what men seek to prove is first assumed.

If the expression means any day of the week, it means the seventh day, which the Bible declares to be the Sabbath of the Lord. This idea comports well with the Jewish character of the Revelation.

If it be not a corruption of the text—made in a book which was late in coming into the Canon—the term Lord's day evidently refers to the "Great and notable Day of the Lord," the time of his coming and judgments, which form the subject matter of the Revelation. A literal rendering of the expression supports this idea—"I was in the Spirit in the Lordly day," or "the day pertaining to the Lord."

We are now prepared to sum up the case as regards the example of Christ and his apostles in observing the first day of the week.

Six passages are quoted in favor of such observance. Only *three* of these passages mention the first day of the week in any manner. Neither of them speaks of it as sabbatic, or as commemorative of any event, or sacred, or to be regarded above other days, and it is only by vague and illogical inferences that either of them is made to produce a shadow of proof for such a change. Concerning the other three, it is only *supposed* by the advocates of the popular theory, that they in some way refer to the first day. To this therefore, does the "argument from example" come, when carefully examined. The New Testament never speaks of, or hints at, a change of the Sabbath; it contains no notice of any commemorative or sabbatic observance of Sunday. It does tell of the repeated and continued observance of the Sabbath by Christ and his Apostles. Will the reader please examine the Bible to see whether these things are so. Sunday observance is a myth, as far as the Bible is concerned, and the theory of a "change of the Sabbath by divine authority," had its birth with English Puritanism less than three hundred years ago.

APPENDIX A.

THE ORIGIN OF THE WEEK.

When did the week originate? This is an important question, both as a fact in history, and as a factor in the Sabbath question. The origin of the week and of the Sabbath which closes it, thus establishing its limit, must be contemporaneous. If the week antedates Judaism, and existed outside the Hebrew nation, the Sabbath is thereby shown to be universal rather than "Jewish." If it antedates Moses, his legislation and leadership, it is not "Mosaic." If the week which antedates Moses and existed among the nations that flourished before the time of the Hebrew nation is identical with the Hebrew and the Christian week, then it is certain that there was no change of the week or of the Sabbath when the Israelites left Egypt, as certain men claim who are more visionary than scholarly. Thus the existence of a primeval and universal week, identical with our own, settles at least three phases of the Sabbath question, without appeal to the Bible.

We give below the results of the latest research on this point, and draw certain conclusions thereon:

BABYLONIA AND ASSYRIA.

"The science of Assyria, like most things else, was derived from Accad. A large number of its technical terms were borrowed from the Turanian, and continued to the last, an enduring monument of the debt owed by the Semite to his predecessor. At the same time, he did not remain a mere imitator; science received a development in his hands which might have been looked for in vain from a Turanian race. First and foremost comes the astronomy, for which Babylonia was so famous in the ancient world. Its beginning goes back to the time when the Accadians had not descended from their mountain fastnesses. The zenith was fixed above Elam, and not above Babylonia, and the 'Mountain of the East,' the primitive home of the race was supposed to support the firmament. The shrines on the topmost terraces of the temples were used also as observatories. Ur had its royal observatory, and so probably had the other cities of Chaldea; in Assyria they existed at Assur, Nineveh, and Arbela, and the astronomers, royal, had to send in their reports to the king twice a month. At an early date the stars were numbered and named; but the most important astronomical work of the Accadians was the formation of a calendar. This came after the division of the heavens into degrees, since the twelve months (of thirty days each) were named after the zodiacal signs, and would seem to belong to about 2200, B. C. Somewhat strangely, the

Accadian calendar appears to have passed to the Assyrians (and through them to the Jews) through the medium of the Aramæans. . . . The week of seven days was in use from an early period, indeed, the names which we still give to the days can be traced to Ancient Babylonia; and the seventh day was one of *sulum*, or 'rest.'"[1]

The *Library of Universal Knowledge* bears the following testimony:

"The dominant people in Babylonia in the earliest times were the Accad or Accadians. They had come originally from the mountains of Elam to the east of the Tigris, and hence their name Accad, which means 'highlanders.' They brought with them the art of cuneiform writing as well as other arts and sciences, especially astronomy. It is in the Turanian language of these Accadians that the cuneiform inscriptions of Babylonia are written for many centuries. And when the Semitic tongue had become predominant, Accadian, now a dead language, was to the Assyrians what Latin has been to the nations of modern Europe. Assyrian scholars translated the Accadian literature into their own language and their technical and sacred terms were borrowed from it. Every day is bringing to light new proofs of the influence of these Accadians upon the civilization of the Semitic nations, and through them upon that of Europe. Greece, it is well known, derived its system of weights and measures from the Babylonian standard; but these have proved to

[1] Encyc. Britannica, Art. "Babylonia," vol. 3, p. 165.

be of Accadian origin. The Greek *mina* or *mna*, the fundamental unit of the Greek monetary system, is the *maneh* of Carchemish, and *maneh* is found to be, not a Semitic, but an Accadian word, showing the origin of the system. The sexagesimal division of the circle, the signs of the zodiac, *a week of seven days, named as we now name them, and the seventh a day of rest*, are all Accadian. Every large city had its public library. In the royal library of a Babylonian monarch, Sargon (about 2000 B. C.), every tablet was numbered so that the reader had only to write down the number of the tablet he wanted and it was handed him by the librarian. Among the multifarious subjects of this extensive literature, are hymns to the gods strikingly like the Hebrew Psalms, and in a long mythological poem there is an episode giving an account of the deluge almost identical with that of Genesis, only more detailed."

The *Presbyterian Review* for October, 1882, contains an article upon "The Sabbath and the Cuneiform Inscriptions," by Prof. Francis Brown, from which the following is extracted:

" In the very first section of the book of Genesis (ii. 2.), God is represented as resting on the seventh day, and in Exodus (xx. 11), the command to observe the Sabbath is based upon God's so resting: Now it became evident, as soon as men were able to study the fundamental notions of the Babylonians and Assyrians, with the help of contemporary documents, that the number *seven* was one of great significance to them. Oppert found in an

Astronomical Tablet a connection between the sun, moon, and five planets, and the days of the week. And Schrader argued at length for the week of seven days as original with the Babylonians. But still earlier than this, George Smith had made an important discovery. He says, 'In the year 1869, I discovered among other things a curious religious calendar of the Assyrians, in which every month is divided into four weeks, and the seventh days or Sabbaths, are marked out as days on which no work should be undertaken.' 'In another place he tells us, more explicitly, that the 7th, 14th, 19th, 21st, and 28th days are described by an idiogram equivalent to *sulu* or *sulum*, meaning rest. The calendar contains lists of works forbidden to be done on these days, which evidently correspond to the Sabbath of the Jews.

"In 1875 appeared the fourth volume of the *Cuneiform Inscriptions of Western Asia*, containing some calendar texts, and in connection with these, Sayce took occasion to confirm the statements of Smith, and gave a translation of the requirements for the seventh day. Here we find also, the first mention of Boscawen's discovery that Sabbattu is in one place explained as *umi nuhlibbi*, 'a day of rest of heart.' In the following year Sayce published a translation of the whole knowledge, or description of the days, of the intercalary month *Elul*, calling special attention to the restrictions imposed for each seventh day. Since then there have been repeated allusions to the 'Babylonian Sabbath,' and some employment of it by a too hasty Apologetics. . . .

"Oppert was the first to call attention to a cuneiform tablet containing a list of stars, seven in number, connected each with a deity, the whole list corresponding to the deities whose names our days bear; the list concludes, according to him, with the words 'These are the seven chiefs of the days of the week (*masi*).' But this translation of *masi* was not accompanied by any proof of its correctness, and Schrader, who took up the general idea of Oppert, wisely sought to lay a firmer foundation. He starts from the position that the Arabians owed the seven day week to the Jews, and that among these and their ancestors, the old Hebrews, it had been known from time immemorial. That the Hebrews did not invent it, appears from the knowledge of it among the ancient Aramæans as well, who can hardly have derived it from the Hebrews; that the Hebrews learned it from the Aramæans is contrary to the Hebrew conception of its remote antiquity among themselves. They could not have learned it in Egypt, for there the 'week' was ten days long. Thus we are pointed back to the early home of the Canaanites (Hebrews and Phenicians) in Babylonia. After thus noticing the historical probability, Schrader then brings in the inscription which Oppert had translated, laying stress upon the order and names of the gods to whom the stars were said to belong: *Shamash*, sun; *Shin*, moon; *Nergal*, Mars, Zivis, (Ti'v); *Nebo*, Mercury, Woden; *Merodach*, Jupiter, Thor; *Ishtar*, Venus, Freia; *Adar*, Saturn. The inference is that the names of the seven week days originated in Babylonia; but if so, the seven-day week must have existed previously to the assignment of the names, and thus we have an explanation of its early appearance among the Hebrews, and also of their habit of numbering instead of naming the days;

for only in comparatively late times (from a period not long, it may be, before the Christian era), does it appear that the *names* of the days were transmitted from people to people along with the week."

The following letter from Prof. Sayce, Deputy Professor of Comparative Philology, Oxford, England, dated Queen's College, Nov. 22, 1875, gives the facts above referred to, in detail, as follows:

"THE CHALDEAN ORIGIN OF THE SABBATH."

"It is now some time since first Mr. Oppert, and then more fully Dr. Schrader,[1] pointed out the Babylonian origin of the week. Seven was a sacred number among the Accadians, and their lunar months were at an early epoch divided into periods of seven days each. The days were dedicated to the sun and moon and five planets, and to the deities who presided over these. The northern Semites borrowed this division of time, and carried it with them on their migration to the West. In one of the newly found fragments which recount the Chaldean Version of the Creation the appointment of the stars called 'leaders of the week,' is expressly mentioned, and the same fragment records how the moon was made ' to go forth from the heaven on the seventh day.'

"Four years ago Mr. Geo. Smith drew attention to the fact that the 7th, 14th, 21st, and 28th days of the month were termed days of *sulum* or 'rest,' on which certain works were forbidden to be done ; and that the expression

[1] *Studien and Kritiken,* 1874.

'day of rest' was but the Assyrian translation of the older Accadian equivalent which signified '*dies nefastus.*' Now a hemerology of the month of the intercalatory Elul, lithographed in the fourth volume of the *Cuneiform Inscriptions of Western Asia*, gives what we may call a Saints Calendar for the month, with notes upon the religious duties required from the king on each day. The memorandum attached to the seventh day, I translate as follows:

" The seventh day, the festival of Merodach and Zirpanitu: a holy day. A Sabbath for the ruler of great nations. *Sodden* flesh (and) cooked fruit he may not eat. His clothes he may not change. (New) garments he may not put on. Sacrifices he may not offer. The king his chariot may not drive. In royal fashion he may not legislate. A place of assembly for the Judge he may not establish. Medicine for his ailments of body he may not apply. ' To make a *measured square* (translated also, To make a *sacred spot*,' which is much more natural and to be preferred) it is suitable. During the (ensuing) night, in the presence of Merodach and Istar, the king should erect his altar, make a sacrifice, and lifting up his hand, worship (in) the high place of the God.

" The same memorandum is attached to the 14th, 21st, and 28th days of the month, except that the 14th was consecrated to Beltis and Nergal, the 21st to the moon and the sun, and the 28th to Hea and Nergal, whose rest day it is expressly stated to be, the word being written in Accadian. On the 21st, moreover, it was 'white garments,' which might not be put on. and the sacrifices to the gods had to be performed at dawn. The 19th day was also a Sabbath, the 'white day' of the Goddess Gula. I have explained in my monograph upon the Babylonian Astronomy (in the *Transactions* of the society of Biblical Archæology, 1874, p. 207) how this came to be the case.

"Even the word *Sabbath* itself was not unknown to the Assyrians. Mr. Boscawen has pointed out to me that it occurs, under the form Sabbattu in W. A. I. 2: 32, 16, where it is explained as a 'day of rest for the heart.'"

The explanation concerning the 19th day of the month, to which Prof. Sayce refers, is as follows:

"The months were lunar and were divided into two lunations; and the days on which the quarters of the moon began, as well as the beginning of the second lunation were called days of *Sulum* or 'rest,' on which certain works were forbidden."[1]

Other authorities speak as follows:

"Among the Semitic nations, which as far as our information goes, seem to have had the computation by weeks from the earliest period, the Arabs stand foremost; and, up to this day, count their days by sevens, beginning and ending with the sunset previous to each new day; and they count them instead of giving them special names, except Friday, which is called 'Day of Assembly,' or Aruba, Eve (of the Jewish Sabbath). Slavonians, Lithuanians and Finns also count their days from Sunday instead of giving them names."[2]

[1] Transactions of the Society of Biblical Archæology, Vol. 3, p. 207.
[2] Chamber's Encyclopedia, Article "Week."

" It (the week) was found as a civil institution in the very earliest times among the Hindoos, Persians, Assyrians, and Egyptians. But the Jews were the only nation with which the week had a religious signification. With the Egyptians, Assyrians, etc., the seventh day was simply a day of recreation; with the Jews it was a day of worship, the Sabbath." [1]

In the article on Sunday, Johnson gives the following definition:

" Sunday [Sax. *Sunnan Darg*. Lat. *Dies Solis*. In the Sanscrit and other languages of India, the first day of the week has the same signification]."

In the *Contemporary Review*, for June, 1879, the astronomer, R. A. Proctor, argues that the moon was probably the first measure of the month; also, that the month and week were used as convenient standards for measuring in business matters, as seen in the case of Jacob and Laban. So he thinks business and religion combined to establish the week. Mr. Proctor adds:

" Be this however as it may, it seems abundantly clear that quite early in the progress of astronomy, the more scientific and observant must have recognized the unfitness of the week as an astronomical measure of time. With the disappearance of the week from astronomical systems (the lunar quarters being retained, however) the week

[1] Johnson's New Universal Encyclopedia, Article " Week."

may be considered to have become what it is now for ourselves, a civil, and in some sense a religious time measure."

This period Mr. Proctor places as early as 2170 B. C.

In a later work, Prof. Proctor supports the antiquity of the week on scientific grounds, in the strongest manner. He sets Revelation aside, and attempts to account for all forms of time measurement on an astrological and astronomic basis. He makes a long *à priori* argument to show how these influences wrought to develop the week as the *first* time measure, and how all succeeding divisions of time followed through the same influences, combined with the religious element. Developing this argument he says:

"In the first place, I think it will appear that some division of the month analogous to the week must have been sugggested as a measure of time long before the year. Commonly the year is taken as either the first and most obvious of all time measure, or else as only second to the day. But in its astronomical aspect the year is not a very obvious division of time. I am not here speaking, be it understood, of the exact determination of the length of the year. That, of necessity, was a work requiring much time, and could only have been successfully achieved by astronomers of considerable skill. I am referring to the commonplace year, the ordinary progression of those celestial phenomena which mark the changes of the seasons. . . . But no definite way of noting the progress of the year by the movements of the sun or stars would probably have suggested itself until some time after the moon's motions had been used as a means of measuring time.

"The lunar changes, on the other hand, are very striking and obvious; they can be readily watched, and they are marked by easily determinable stages. It appears more easy, says Whewell, and in earlier stages of civilization (it was) more common, to count time by *moons* than by years."[1]

In developing his argument, Prof. Proctor concludes that *lunar* astronomy with the week as the chief measure of time prevailed a long time before *solar* astronomy and the year were known. He thinks that the change came at a point where the origin of the science of astronomy has been assumed to be, with the Chaldeans, and that " As to the epoch of the real beginning of astronomy we have no means of judging." The Chaldean epoch, when the solar year came in, he claims, could not have been the beginning or even during the infancy of the science. This epoch Prof. Proctor places at about 2170 B. C. So that, scientifically considered, the origin of the week is much earlier than that date.

The chapter on the "Origin of the Week" is followed by one on "Saturn and the Sabbath of the

[1] The Great Pyramid, pp. 204, 206. London: 1883.

Jews." In the former chapter (p. 217), Mr Proctor claims that, "The earliest record we have of hiring is that contained in Genesis xxix," when the service of Jacob with Laban is regulated by the week and month. Still, with an inconsistency not wholly uncommon, he claims that the Sabbath was borrowed by the Hebrews from the Egyptians and Chaldeans. He says:

"Assigning the origin of the first Jewish observance of the Sabbath to the time of the Exodus, we are forced to the conclusion that the custom of keeping each seventh day as a day of rest, was derived from the people amongst whom the Jews had been sojourning more than two hundred years. It is unreasonable to suppose that Moses would have added to the almost overwhelming difficulties which he had to encounter in dealing with the obstinate people he led from Egypt, the task of establishing a new festival. Such a task is at all times difficult, but at the time of the Exodus it would have been hopeless to undertake it. The people were continually rebelling against Moses, because he sought to turn them from the worship of the gods of Egypt, in whom they were disposed to trust. It was no time to establish a new festival, unless one could be devised which should correspond with the customs they had learned in Egypt. Moses would seem indeed to have pursued a course of compromise. Opposing manfully the worship of the Egyptian gods, he adopted, nevertheless, Egyptian ceremonies and festivals, only so far modifying them that (as he explains them)

ORIGIN OF THE WEEK. 103

they ceased to be associated with the worship of false gods.

"We have also historical evidence as to the non-Jewish origin of the observance of the seventh day as decisive of the arguments I have been considering. For Philo Judæus, Josephus, Clement of Alexandria and others, speak plainly of the week as not of Jewish origin, but common to all the Oriental nations."[1]

In farther corroboration of the fact that the primeval week was closed by the Sabbath, in the same order as at present, Mr. Proctor says:

"I must remark, however, that this point is by no means essential for the main argument of this paper, which is in reality based on the unquestioned fact that amongst all the nations which used the week as a division of time, the seventh day was associated with the planet Saturn."[2]

Mr. Proctor also labors to show that all the Jewish festivals were the product of Sabaism and astrology as they prevailed among the Pagan nations, and that Moses developed the Jewish system as a general compromise between his own religious notions and the practices which the Hebrews had become accustomed to in Egypt. He ignores the Patriarchal period and its influence. In short, he

[1] pp. 248—9.
[2] Pyramid, etc., p. 254.

accepts the facts concerning the primeval and universal character of the week, but attempts to account for it on non-Biblical grounds. We deem it far more logical, and the only conclusion consistent with Christian faith, that the week was established at the earliest period by the Sabbath as the sacred time-measure. The Patriarchal and Hebrew line of humanity retained the true conception, and the true naming of the days, that is by numerals. The other lines of humanity drifted away from this primeval revelation, adopted the worship of the heavenly bodies, and named the days of the week after the planets. They preserved the original order of the days, and hence whenever the two lines of human life touch each other in history, God's Sabbath and Saturn's day coincide. In the apostatizing of the nations, sun worship and the sun god became the great rival of Jehovah, and the sun's day, for thousands of years, has been the one great rival of God's Sabbath. But the ripening centuries are hastening the time when God and his Sabbath will be vindicated, and re-enthroned, and not least among the influences at work toward this end are the deductions of science and history, which prove the primeval and universal existence of the week, in its present and unbroken order.

The *Philological Museum* assigns the names of the days of the week to the mythology of the Scandinavians, the astrology of the Egyptians and Chaldeans, and the mythology of the Romans, combined. It also states that "Saturn's day was always connected with the Jewish Sabbath," which it is claimed is not absurd, because plainly the week was ancient.[1]

IDELER, thinks the Romans saw some connection between the Jewish Sabbath and their Saturn-alia. He also recognizes the existence of the Sabbath, the seventh day, among the Gentile nations before the Roman era.[2]

A work by JOHN BRADY, London, entitled *Clavis Calendarium*, also recognizes the universal and primeval character of the week.[3]

These testimonies combine to show that the week, as now numbered and named, existed from the remotest period yet reached among the Accadians, Babylonians, and Assyrians.

INDIA.

There is abundant testimony to the existence of the week among the people of India also, where perhaps the astronomical element was most strongly marked.

[1] Vol. 1, p. 28
[2] Chronology, vol. 2, pp. 175, 178.
[3] Vol. 1, pp. 95, 96.

Mr. Wilson inclines to the opinion that the knowledge of the week may have originated in India. We think that it did not originate in Egypt, but with the Accadian ancestors of the Babylonians. The following are Mr. Wilson's words:

"The specification of the days of the week by the names of the seven planets, is, as it is well known, familiar to the Hindus. The origin of this is not very precisely ascertained, as it was unknown to the Greeks, and not adopted by the Romans until a later period. It is commonly ascribed to the Egyptians and Babylonians, but on no very sufficient authority, and the Hindus appear to have at least as good a title as any other people to the invention.

. . . Aditya-Vara, Ravi-Vara, or Rabi-Bar, in the barbarized vernacular, Dies Solis, Sunday is one of every seven. This is somewhat different from the Seventh Tithi, or lunar day; but a sort of sanctity is or was attached even to Sunday, and fasting on it was considered obligatory or meritorious. . . . It is impossible to avoid inferring from the general character of the prayers and observances and the sanctity evidently attached to the recurring seventh day, some connection with the Sabbath, or Seventh of the Hebrew Heptameron." [1]

Witness also the following:

"Whoever listens to the story of Prahlada is immedi-

[1] H. H. Wilson, A. M., F. R. S., Professor of Sanscrit, Oxford, Works, vol. 2, of Essays on the Religion of the Hindus, pp. 198—201.

ately cleansed from his sins; the iniquities that he commits by night or by day, shall be expiated by once hearing, or once reading the history of Prahlada. The perusal of this history on the day of full moon, of new moon, or on the eighth or twelfth day of the lunation shall yield fruit equal to the gift of a cow," [*i. e.*, a great gift]. Note. "The days of full and new moon are sacred with all sects of Hindus."[1]

In *Sacred Books of the East* (Max Muller) vol. 2, p. 85, we find fasting on full and new moon, as a penance for sin. In vol. 5, p. 406, Mr. Muller says:

"The first weekly period begins with a day dedicated to Anharmazd, and called by his own name; and each of the three other weekly periods also begins with a day dedicated to Anharmazd, but called by the name of Din, religion, with the name of the following day added as a cognomen. The first week therefore consists of the day of Anharmazd, followed by six days named after the six archangels, respectively. The second week consists of the day Din-with-ataro, followed by six days named after the angels of fire water, the sun, the moon, Mercury, and the primeval ox. The third week consists of the day Din-with-Mitro, followed by seven days named after the angels of solar light, obedience and justice, the guardian spirits and the angels of victory, pleasure and wind. And the fourth week consists of the day Din-with-Dino, followed by seven days named after the angels of religion, right-

[1] Vishnu Purana, chap. 20, Wilson's Trans.

eousness, rectitude, the sky, the earth, the liturgy, and the fixed stars."

Here we have the week, with the days named in order though the month, and two weeks of eight days to meet the intercalary difficulty. It is the Hebrew week, modified by the astronomical element. The Sabbatic division of the Buddhist week is also seen by the following, which dates from the 4th century B. C.:

"In the first place, Ananda, when the Great King of Glory, on the Sabbath-day, on the day of the full moon, had purified himself, and had gone up into the upper story of his palace to keep the sacred day, there then appeared to him the heavenly 'Treasure of the Wheel,' with its nave, its tire, and all its spokes complete.

"When he beheld it, the Great King of Glory thought: This saying have I heard; when a king of the warrior race, an anointed king, has purified himself on the Sabbath-day, on the day of full moon, and has gone up into the upper story of his palace to keep the sacred day, if there appear to him the heavenly 'Treasure of the Wheel,' . . . that king becomes a king of kings invincible."

In foot-notes we have the following:

"1. Uposatha is the name for the sacred day of the moon's changes—first and more especially the fullmoon day; next the new-moon day; and lastly the days equidistant between these two. It was therefore a weekly sacred day, and as Childers says: may often be well rendered Sabbath." "2. Uposatha, a weekly sacred day; being full-moon day, new-moon day, and two equidistant intermediate days." [1]

Concerning the origin of the week, Max Muller says:

"It is well known that the names of the seven days of the week are derived from the names of the planets, and it is equally well known that in Europe the system of weeks and week days is comparatively of very modern origin. It was not a Greek, nor a Roman, nor a Hindu, but a Jewish or Babylonian invention." [2]

The following, corresponds with Mr. Muller's conclusions, and with the facts already presented:

"Throughout all the nations of the ancient world the planets are to be found appropriated to the days of the week. The seven-day cycle with each day named after a planet, and universally the same day allotted to the same planet in all the nations of the world, constitute the first proof and leave no room to doubt that one system must have prevailed over the whole." [3]

CHINA.

The knowledge of the week was transferred through India to China, as is shown by the following:

"These planets with the sun and moon, form the

[1] Buddhist Suttas, Sacred Books of the East, vol. 12, pp. 251, 254.
[2] Chips from a German Workshop, vol. 5, p. 116.
[3] Godfry Higgin's Anaclypsis, Book 1, chap. 1 sec. 5.

'seven bright celestial objects.' They constitute the mythological week of seven days, which sprang up in Babylonia and spread to India, and also through Europe, in the days of the Roman Empire."

"Some Chinese almanacs call Sunday the day of Mrit, the 'Persian Mithras, a name for the sun."

... In the 'Peacock Sutra' the days of the week are also given."[1]

It is befitting to close this line of testimony by the following from high authority, which has been translated especially for this chapter. President Goguet of France, speaking of the week, says:

"We find from time immemorial, the use of this period among all nations without any variation in the form of it. The Israelites, Assyrians, Egyptians, Indians, Arabians, and, in a word, all the nations of the Orient, have, in all ages, made use of a week of seven days. We find the same custom among the ancient Romans, Gauls, Britons, Germans, the nations of the North, and America. Many vain conjectures have been formed concerning the reason and motives which determined all mankind to agree in this primitive division of time; but it is evident that the tradition concerning the length of time employed in the creation of the world has given rise to this usage, universal and immemorial, which originally divided the week into seven days."[2]

[1] *Chinese Buddhism*, by Joseph Edkins, D. D., p. 211. Tubners Oriental Series.

[2] *De L'Origine Des Loix, Des Arts, et Des Sciences*, (Origin Of Laws, etc.,)—Vol. 1, Book chap. 2, p. 217, Paris, 1758.

The following conclusions are inevitable from the foregoing facts:

1. The week of seven days is one of the older if not the oldest of the universal institutions of human society.

2. The original week of the Accadians and other Asiatic nations is identical with the Ancient week of the Hebrews, which is shown to have existed previously to the enslavement in Egypt, by the pre-Mosaic history, as given in the Old Testament—see Gen. ii. 2; vii. 4; viii. 10, 12. It also appears in the observance of the Sabbath *before* the giving of the Decalogue. See Ex. xvi. The seventh day of the Accadian and Babylonian week was a "day of rest," and was identical with the Sabbath. This indicates a primeval and universal Revelation concerning the Sabbath, which, combined with the astronomical element, gave the universal week.

3. The original Hebrew week has been kept intact until the present time. All the theories concerning Sunday as related to the Sabbath question are based upon the fact that it is the *first day of the Hebrew week*. This identity of the ancient and modern week shows that the Sabbath and the week are both much older than Judaism. Certain writers are very persistent in claiming that the order of the week has

been broken up by changes that have taken place in the civil calendar, and that the identity of the days of the week cannot be preserved, because of variations in longitude. To meet these objections we add the following facts :

European countries borrowed their calendar from the Romans. In the pre-historic period, under Romulus, the year is said to have been divided into ten months, aggregating 304 days. How the other days were disposed of is not known. Numa Pompilius, the second king of Rome, added two months, January at the beginning, and February at the end of the year. About 450 B. C., under the Decemvirs, February was taken from the end of the year, and placed next after January. Under this arrangement the month was made to consist of 29 and 30 days, alternately, to accord with the lunar changes, giving a sum total of 354 days in the year; one day was added to this to make the number more "fortunate." This lunar year was found to be less than the solar year by at least ten days. To remedy this, Numa added an intercalary month once in two years, of 22 and 23 days alternately, thus giving 1, 465 days in four years, or an average of $366\frac{1}{4}$ days in a year. Complete harmony between the lunar and the civil year was not yet attained, and hence it was ordered that every third period of eight years should have only three intercalary months of 22 days each. This gave an average year of 365¼ days. The regulating of the calendar thus established was left to the Pontiffs, who made political capital by intercalating irregularly, so as to affect the elections, and other events, until in the time of Julius Cæsar the difference between the civil and the lunar year amounted to three months; autumn came in summer, and winter came in autumn. To remedy this, Julius abolished the lunar year, and attempted to harmonize the civil year and the solar by the following method. He fixed the civil year at three hundred and sixty-five and one fourth days, every fourth year having three hundred and sixty-six. The first Julian year was reckoned from Jan. 1, 46 B. C.; our civil calendar begins at that point. In this rearrangement under Julius, January, March, May, July, September, and November each had thirty-one days; the rest had thirty each, except February, which had twenty-nine, with an added day every fourth year. When Augustus became emperor, he demanded that his month, August, should have as many days as July, the month of Julius; hence a day was taken from February and given to August; then, that three months of thirty-one days each might not succeed each other, September and November were reduced to thirty days, each, and October and December were increased to thirty-one. On such childish grounds were some of the changes made.

These changes did not remove all trouble. Astronomical science was not then able to measure the solar year accurately, and the civil year was accepted as being eleven minutes and fourteen seconds too long. It was even more than this, and in a few centuries the vernal equinox shifted from the twenty-fifth to the eleventh of March. In 1582, Pope Gregory XIII. sought to correct this error by dropping ten days from the civil calendar. Gregory also ordered that the intercalation of one day in each year divisible by four should extend to the centurial years, as well as others. Such have been the changes in the calendar. They have all been made to harmonize the *civil year* with the *solar year*. Not one of them has touched the week. Every one knows that the addition of one day each leap year does not affect the week.

LONGITUDE.

In the matter of longitude, the case is simple when not complicated by erroneous conceptions. The days travel around the earth, as a ship or a man does, retaining their identity and reaching each degree of longitude in due time. As a simple illustration, take the following: Richard Doe starts from New York to go westward, on the 11th day of August 1884, at sunrise. The man and the day leave New York together. But the day outruns the man, and reaches Chicago in an hour, while Doe comes in much later. No one complained of the day because it did not reach Chicago at the same hour it did New York. The day could not be in New York and Chicago at the same time any more than the man could. When the day did reach Chicago or San Francisco, everybody hailed it as the 11th day of August, the identical day that it was in New York, just as Doe's friends hailed him on his arrival. No day exists at a given degree of longitude *until* it reaches that point. In the case supposed the day was the 224th of the year, the 11th of the month, and the 2d of the week. This identity was retained in all its course, at Chicago, Omaha, etc. It will be seen by this illustration that the identity of each day is kept as certainly as the identity of a man is retained. If the loss of identity could occur in the case of the Sabbath, it would occur equally with every other day in the week the month, or the year. No such disorder is ever suspected in social, or business life. No hint of such disorder is heard except in connection with the Sabbath question, and then only as a means of breaking the force of the truth that the seventh day of each week in its regular succession is the Sabbath. Commerce and science have agreed to correct the discrepancy which occurs when the circle of the earth is completed in circumnavigation, by fixing the "Day line" at a given point in the Pacific ocean, where the movements of the circumnavigator and of the sun are made to harmonize.

Have the week and the Sabbath come to us in regular succession, and in unbroken order?

The Sabbath measures the week in all Biblical history. The week is fully recognized during the Patriarchal period, previous to the giving of the law, (See Gen. vii. 10, and xix. 27,) and when the law was given (Ex. xx.) God connected the Sabbath directly with his own example at the close of the creative week. It is hence legitimate to conclude that the Sabbath measured the week before the giving of the law, as it did after.

It is impossible to believe that God deceived the Israelites at Sinai, by founding the Sabbath on his own example, and then designating a day not in the regular order from the Adamic Sabbath. It would have been sheer deception thus to do. The Sabbath law rested on a false foundation from the beginning, if the day designated in the law was not the true one, and God was the immediate author of the cheat. The proposition destroys itself.

From the giving of the law at Sinai to the coming of Christ, the Israelites retained the Sabbath in unbroken order; their history has no trace of confusion on this point. From the time of Christ to the present, the Jews, scattered in all lands, have maintained the observance of the Sabbath, with the same unbroken regularity. Thus we have a continuous chain from the present date to Sinai, and thence to Creation, through a people whose tenacity of national life, manners and customs, has been the wonder of the centuries. This preservation of the historic Sabbath of Jehovah is not the least important part of their wondrous mission and unfulfilled work.

Christ, who is the center of all dispensations, recognized the Sabbath as a part of his Father's law and pruned it that it might bring forth more and better fruit.

Since the middle of the second century of the Christian era, the first, third, fourth and sixth days of this same week, *measured by this same Sabbath*, have been observed to commemorate certain events, said to have occurred on these days of the week. During all this time, no lover of the Wednesday or the Friday fast, or of the Sunday festival, has ever doubted that he was observing these days in their regular weekly order and succession.

To summarize, we have the following proofs: At Sinai, God gave the Sabbath law and designated a day, which he founded upon his own example, thus linking it with the "Adamic Sabbath." That day in its regular order, the Jews still keep. For the last sixteen hundred years, Wednesday, Friday, and Sunday, have been observed in some form, in their weekly order, by so many persons as to make it impossible for any disturbance to take place in the calendar of the week, without leaving traces on almost every page of the history of the church.

These facts give all needful logical and historical support to the claim that the seventh day of the week, improperly called "Saturday," is the Sabbath of Jehovah, in regular succession from the hour when the morning stars sang together and the Sons of God shouted for joy.

from him that there are 104 dialects distributed among, and dependent upon, the fifty-two languages given in the Table. The reader will find the table prepared by the Prince, of special interest.

For the Assyrian text and the Targum of Onkelos we are indebted to Mr. E. A. Budge, whose articles on Assyrian archæology are valuable contributions to our paper.

Our thanks are due to the Rev. Dr. L. Lœwe for the Circassian list of days, which he heard from the mouths of the natives themselves, and for valuable remarks which will be found in the Notes.

Thanks are also due to the Rev. Albert Lowy for statements respecting the Hebrew and the Targum dialect; to the editor of the *Jewish Chronicle* for confirmation of certain Jewish customs; and to Dr. Birch of the British Museum for assistance in the Coptic.

Much valuable aid has been rendered in our Armenian studies by Mr. Krikor H. Shahinian, of Amasia, Asia Minor, formerly a student of the American College, Constantinople; and further confirmation of matters in our researches in Arabian literature has been given by Mr. N. Giamaal, of Acre, Palestine, a Syrian acquaintance of former years."

1. It will be seen that the Oriental conception of the Sabbath makes it the chief or supporting day. All other days lean on it; all proceed towards it.

2. Note that Samstag Samedi, Sabbato, etc., are the exact counterpart of *Sabbath*, and not of Saturday.

3. The following from the pen of Doctor Jones, to the writer is worth repeating:

"In Malagasy, Japanese, the languages of the Caucasus, of eastern Kurdistan, Thibet, Burmah; in west and east Africa, and central also, in the fifty-two European languages and nearly four hundred dependent dialects, we have a complete chronological account of the sacred seven days, from the earliest historic times. Man has tampered with the year and with the months, but he has never been anxious to change the week from seven to any other number; and whatever attempt has been made in that direction, has signally failed. Protestantism has attempted a change of the Sabbath, but that said attempt is of puny man, the Table of Days is a swift witness. The *uses* of these languages in all ages and countries *are in accord* and therefore admit of no contradiction. They speak the truth, the whole truth, and nothing but the truth."

We have the right to ask a careful study of the question of the origin and identity of the week, by every reader. It is an important element in the Sabbath controversy. The facts which are here set forth, are a complete answer to the claim that the Sabbath and the week began with the Hebrew nation and the legislation of Moses. These facts answer with equal positiveness the still more visionary notion that the Sabbath was changed at the exodus of the Israelites from Egypt, and that hence, the first day of the week is the original seventh day. These facts also show that "The Sabbath" is the definite proper name of a specific day of the week; and hence that it is futile to assert that "The Sabbath," and "A Sabbath" are equivalents, or that the Sabbath is any one day of the week which the choice of man may indicate. The facts herein set forth, form a permanent barrier against all similar theories, and hold us down to the one truth of the ages, and of the fourth commandment: "The seventh day is the Sabbath of the Lord thy God."

We have selected representative languages from the different families, modifying the family arrangement somewhat under the head of Japhetic Group, in order to retain a certain important geographical connection among the European languages.

Those who desire to pursue this line of investigation further are referred to the Chart by Dr. Jones, which gives about twice the number of languages for which we have space, and prints each in its native text.

I.—SEMITIC GROUP

LANGUAGES.	WEEK.	1	2	3	4	5	6	7
Hebrew Bible.	sha-vu-ah. Seven.	yom e-khad. Day one.	yom she-ni. Day 2d.	yom she-li-shi. Day Third.	yom re-vii. Day Fourth.	yom kha-mi-shi. Day Fifth.	yom hash-shi-shi. Day the 6th.	yom hash-she-vi-i. Day the 7th or yom hash-shab-bath. Day the Sabbath.
Hebrew. Ancient & modern use.	sha-vu-ah. Seven.	e-khad be-shab-bath. one; into the Sabbath.	she-ni be-shab-bath. 2d into the Sabbath.	she-li-shi be-shab-bath. 3d into the Sabbath.	re-vi-i be-shab-bath. 4th into the Sabbath.	kha-mi-shi be-shab-bath. 5th into the Sabbath.	e-reb shab-bath ko-desh. Eve of holy Sabbath.	shab-bath. Sabbath.
Targum of Onkelos.	sha-vu-ah. Seven.	yom khad. Day one.	yom tin-yan. Day 2d.	yom t'-li-thai. Day Third.	yom r'vi-ai. Day 4th.	yom kh'-mi-shai. Day Fifth.	yom sh-thi-thai. Day Sixth.	yom sh'-vi-aa. or Sab-bath.
Targum Dialect of the Jews in Kurdistan.	sha-vu-ah. Seven.	yoy-met khoy-she ba. Day one of the Seven.	yoy-met ti-ru-sheb. Day 2d of the Seven.	yoy-met te-la-wu-sheb. Day 3d of the Seven.	yoy-met ar-bu-sheb. Day 4th of the Seven.	yoy-met kham-shu-sheb. Day 5th of the Seven.	yoy-met a-roy-ta. Day of Eve (of Sabbath.)	yoy-met sha-bat ko-desh. Holy Sabbath Day.
Ancient Syriac.	shab-ba-tho. Sabbath.	khad be-shab-bo. One into Sabbath.	tren be-shab-bo. Two into Sabbath.	ti-lo-tho be-shab-bo. Three into Sabbath.	ar-ba-oh be-shab-bo. Four into Sabbath.	kham-sho be-shab-bo. Five into Sabbath.	e-ruv-tho. Eve (of Sabbath).	shab-ba-tho Sabbath.

SEMITIC GROUP.—Continued.

Chaldee Syriac vul. Pronun.	yu-mat shap-tu. days into Sabbath.	khad be-shab-ba. One into Sabbath.	tren be-shab-ba. Two into Sabbath.	te-la-tha be-shab-ba. Three into Sabbath.	ar-ba be-shab-ba. Four into Sabbath.	kham-sha be-shab-ba. Five into Sabbath.	e-ruv-tho, and ro-ta. Eve of Sabbath.	shap-ta. Sabbath.
Samaritan.	sha-vu-ah. Seven.	yo-ma kha-da. Day One.	yo-ma t'ni-na. Day 2d.	yo-ma t'li-tha. Day Third.	yo-ma re-vi-ah. Day 4th.	yo-ma kha-ni-sha. Day Fifth.	yo-ma she-thi-tha. Day Sixth.	yo-ma ha-she-vi-ah. Day the 7th. Shab-bath
Arabic.	al-as-bu-ah. jum-at. The Seven, Col. (of days).	al-a-had. The One (day).	al-ith-nin. The Two.	ath tha-la-tha. The Three.	al-ar-ba. The Four.	al-kha-mis. The Fifth.	al-jum-at. Assembly (day).	as-sabt. The Sabbath.
Amharic, *Abyssinia*.	sa-me-net. Eight.	e-hud. One.	sa-gna. Second.	mak-sa-gna Third.	re-bu-eh. Fourth.	ha-mus. Fifth.	ar-be. Eve of Sabbath.	san-bat. Sabbath.
Falasha, *Abyssinia*.	sa-me-net.	Ad. One.	San. Second.	Seles. Third.	Loba. Fourth.	Hams. Fifth.	Sedast Kan. Sixth.	Yini San-bat. The Sabbath.
Assyrian.	ma-a-su. Quarter of a lunation.	makh-ru. First.	Sa-an-nu. Second.	sal-sa-al. Third.	ri-bu. Fourth.	kha-an-sa. Fifth.	si-is-su. Sixth.	si-bu-u. Seventh. Sa-ba-tu.

II.—HAMITIC GROUP.

Anc. Egyptian.	No word for week.	Ra. Sun.	Thoth. Chons. Moon.	(Hor going backwards). Mars.	(Sebkau.) Mercury.	Hor ap Sheta. Jupiter.	At-hor. Venus.	Seb. Saturn.
Coptic. *Egypt.*	pi anan, z. A period of time belonging to the Sabbath.	pi ehoou emnah. a. ouai. The 1st Day.	pi ehoou emnah b snau. The 2d Day.	pi ehoou emnah g shomt. The 3d Day.	pi ehoou emnah d ftou. The 4th Day.	pi ehoou emnah e tion. The 5th Day.	pi ehoou emnah—so-ou. The 6th Day.	pi ehoou emnah z shashaf. The 7th Day or Pi Sabbaton.
Galla, *Abyssinia.*	Torbo. Seven.	Sanbata Gadda. Festival Sabbath.	Hu-tshi Duru. 1st Trade Day.	Hu-tshi-la ma-fu. 2d Trade Day.	Robi. Fourth (*day*).	Kams. Fifth (*day*).	Tshi-ma-ta Assembly (*day*).	San-ba ta Tenna. Little Sabbath.

III.—JAPHETIC GROUP.

Sanscrit	Saptaha. Seven.	Bhanu-var. Sun-day.	Soma-var. Moon-day.	Mangal-var. Mars-day.	Budh-var. Mercury-day.	Brihuspati-var. Jupitar-day.	Shukra-var. Venus' Star.	Shani-var Saturn-day.
Hindi.	Suptah. Seven.	Rubi-var. Sun-day.	Som-war. Moon-day.	Kuj. Mars day.	Budh-war. Mercury day.	Guru-war. Jupiter-day.	Shukr-war. Venus-day.	Shuni-war. Saturn-day.

III.—JAPHETIC GROUP.—Continued.

Urdu or Hindustani. (Three names for week, and two names for the days.)	Haftah. Seven. Asbu-ah. Seven. Atwara. Sun-day.	Yek-shamba. One to Sabbath. Atwar. Sunday.	Du-shamba. 2d to Sabbath. Pir. Moon-day.	Sah-shamba. Three to Sabbath. Mangal. Mars.	Cha-har-shamba. Four to Sabbath. Budha. Mercury.	Panj-shamba. 5th to Sabbath. Junarat. Eve (of) Juma.	Jum-a. Assembly (day). Jum-a.	Sanichar. Saturn. Shamba. Sabbath.
Bengali. India.	Saptaha. Seven.	Rabi-var. Sun-day.	Som-bar. Moon-day.	Mangal-bar. Mars-day.	Budha-bar. Mercury-day.	Brihespati-bar. Jupiter-day.	Shukra-bar. Venus-day.	Shani-bar. Saturn-day.
Armenian.	shapat. Sabbath.	min shapti. One to the Sabbath.	yergu-shapti. 2d to the Sabbath.	yerek shapti. 3d to the Sabbath.	chorek shapti. 4th to the Sabbath.	hink shapti. Fifth of the Sabbath.	urpat. Fast Day.	Shapat. Sabbath.

Pashto, *Afghanistan*.	al-isbuah. The seven.	yek-shamba. One to the Sabbath.	du-shamba. Two to Sabbath.	sha-shamba. Three to Sabbath.	char-shamba. Four to Sabbath.	punj-shamba. Five to Sabbath.	jum-ah Assembly (*day*).	shamba. Sabbath. Unemployed day.
Persian.	hafta. Seven (*days*).	yek-shambih. One to Sabbath.	du shambih. Two to Sabbath.	sih-shambih. Three to Sabbath.	chohar-shambih. Four to Sabbath.	panj-shambih. Five to Sabbath.	adina. Religious (*day*).	shambih. Sabbath or Holiday.
Turkish.	asbu-ah. Seven.	bazzar-guni. Market Day.	bazzar irteci. Morrow after Market.	sa-li Third (*day*).	char shamba. Four to Sabbath.	panj-shamba. Five to Sabbath.	jum-a Assembly (*day*).	yom-es-sabt. Day the Sabbath.
Malayan. (*Polynesian*).	Jumat Collection (*of days*).	harlahad. Day One.	hari isnein. Day Two.	haeri thalatha. Day Three.	hari arbaa. Day Four.	hari khamis. Day Fifth.	hari-Jum-at. Assembly day.	hari sabtu. Day Sabbath.

III.—JAPHETIC GROUP.—Continued.

	Aste.	Igande.	Astelen.	Asteartc.	Asteazken.	Ostegun.	Ostiral.	Larumbat one quarter (of the moon or lunation)
Basque. Spain and France.								
Finnish. Finland.	Vilkko	Sunnuntai	Maanantai	Tiistai	Keskiviikko	Tuorstai, Torstai	Porjantai	Lauvantai, corruption of laugurdagur. q. v.
Esthonian. Baltic Russia.	Nadal	Puha-paaw	Esmas-paaw	Telsi-paaw	Kolma-paaw, kesk-nadal	Nelja-paaw	Reede	Lau-paaw (Bath-day)

SABBATH AND SUNDAY.

Livonian. (BalticRussia).	Nadiil	Puva-paava	Eezom-paava	Tuoisna-paava	Kuolmond-paava	Nellond paava	Breitlg, Breedig	Puol-paava Half-day.
Lap. Norway.	Vakko	Sodnu-bæ-ive	Vuosarg	Manebarg	Gaskvakko	Doresdak	Bærjadak, Fasto-bæ-ivve	Lavardak Corruption of Icelandic laugardagur
Permian. (Russia).	Sim-lun, Nedil	Vovzem, Krescene	Vil-vun		Sreda	Cetvertok	Petnica	Subota. Sabbath.
Votiak. Russia.	Arna	Zuc-arna, Arna-nunal	Zuc-arna-bore	Vordys-kon-nunal	Vir-nunal	Pokci arna, Cetvertok-nunal	Biger arra-nunal, Patnica	Kos-nunal, Dry-day (day without work) Sumat, Subbota (Sabbath)
Tsheremis-sian. Russia.	Arna	Rus-arna	Shazma	Koskozam	Vir-ketsha	Iz-arnja	Kog-arnja	Kuks-ketsha. Dry-Day. (day without work).
Morduin. Russia.	Nedlja	Nedlja, Nedlja tshi, Targa tshi	Ponedelj-nik	Vtornik	Sereda	Cetverk	Pjatnica, Pjatsja	Subbota, Subta Sabbath.

III.—JAPHETIC GROUP.—Continued.

	Ilet	Vasarnap	Hetfo	Kedd	Szerda	Csotortok	Pentek	Szombat (Sabbath).
Hungarian (Hungary)	Ilet	Vasarnap	Hetfo	Kedd	Szerda	Csotortok	Pentek	Szombat (Sabbath).
Vogul (Russia).	Sat	Jelping-katel	Sat-ponk-katel	Mot-katel	Kormlt-katel	Nelit-katel	Atit-katel	Katit-katel.
Gaelic. Ireland.	Seachdm-hain	Domlnach	Dia Luain	Dia Mairt, Mairt	Dia cea-dlaoine, Ceadaoin	Dia dar-daoin, Dardaoin	Aoine, Dia haoine	Sathurn, Dia Sath-uirn Saturn, day of Sat-urn
Welsh Wales	Wythnos	Dydd Sul	Dydd Llun	Dydd Ma-wrth	Dydd Mer-cher	Dydd Iau	Dydd Gwener	Dydd Sad-wrn (Day Sat-urn)
Cornish Cornwall (d).	Seithun	De Zil	De Lin	De Merh	De Marhar	De Jeu	De Guenar	De Zadarn (Day Sat-urn)

Breton France.	Sizun	Sul, Disul-Lun, Di-lun	Meurs, Dimeurs	Merc'her, Dimerc'h-er	Iaou, Diz-iou, Diz-iaou	Gwener, Digwener	Sadorn, Disadorn (Saturn, day-Saturn).
Albanian Turkish Albania.	Jave	Dibe	Hane	Marte	Merkure	Eeyte	Premte	Shetune (Saturn).
Greek Greece (d)	Ἑβδομάς	Κυριακή	Τῆς Σελή-νης	Τοῦ Ἄρεως	Τοῦ Ἑρμοῦ	Τοῦ Διὸς ἡμέ-ρα	Τῆς Ἀφροδί-της ἡμέρα	Σάββατον Sabbath
Modern Greek Greece	Ἑβδομάς Ἑβδομάδα	Κυριακή	Δευτέρα	Τρίτη	Τετράδη	Πέμπτη	Παρα-σκευή	Σάββατον Sabbath
Latin Italy (d)	Hebdomas	Dies Solis, Dies Do-minicus, -ca	Dies Lu-næ	Dies Mar-tis	Dies Mer-curii	Dies Jovis	Dies Ven-eris	Sabbatum, Dies Sat-urni Sabbath, day of Sat-urn.

III.—JAPHETIC GROUP.—Continued.

Italian. (Italy).	Settimana	Domenica	Lunedì	Martedì	Mercoledì	Giovedì	Venerdì	Sabato, Sabbato, Sabbath.
Spanish. (Spain).	Semana	Domingo	Lunes	Martes	Miercoles	Jueves	Viernes	Sabado (Sabbath).
Portuguese. (Portugal).	Semana	Domingo	Segunda feira	Terca feira	Quarta feira	Quinta feira	Sexta feira	Sabbado (Sabbath).
French. (France).	Semaine	Dimanche	Lundi	Mardi	Mercredi	Jeudi	Vendredi	Samedi Sabbath day.
Roman. (Spain, Catalonia.)	Semmana	Dlumenge	Dilhins	Dimars	Dimecres	Dijous	Divendres	Dissapte Day-Sabbath.
Rhetian. Canton des Grisons, Switzerland.	Jamna, Emna	Dumeingia	Lindischgis	Marsgis	Mezziamna, Mezemna	Gicvgia	Vendergis	Sonda *Corruption of Sonnabend, q.v*
Wallachian. Roumania or Wallachia.	Septamana	Duminica	Luni	Martsi	Miercuri	Joi	Vineri	Sambata Sabbath.

SABBATH AND SUNDAY.

		Sunday	Monday	Tuesday	Wednesday	Thursday	Friday	Saturday
Old High German (d) South Germany.	Wecha	Sunnun tag	Manetag	Ziestac	Mittawecha	Toniris tac	Friadag	Sunun abaud, Sambaztag (1) Sun(day's)eve; (2) Sabbath's day
Old Low German (d) North Germany.	Wica	Sunun dag						
Anglo Saxon. (d) England.	Wice, Weoce, Wuce, Wecce	Sunnan dæg	Monan dæg	Tiwes dæg	Wodnes dæg	Thunres dæg	Frige dæg	Saternesdæg Saterdæg (1)Saturn's day; (2)Saturday
Friesian. (d) Holland	Wike	Sunnandi.	Monandi	Tiesdi	Wernisdei	Thunresdi	Frigendi	Saterdi, Saturday.
High German. Germany.	Woche	Sonntag	Montag	Dienstag	Mittwoch, —che	Donnerstag	Freitag	Sonnabend Samstag (1) Sun(day's)eve; (2) Sabbath's day

III.—JAPHETIC GROUP.—Continued.

	Week	Sunday	Maandag	Dingsdag	Midweek	Donnerdag	Freedag	Sunnabend Sun(day's) eve
Low German. North Germany (Holstein).	Week	Sundag	Maandag	Dingsdag	Midweek	Donnerdag	Freedag	Sunnabend Sun(day's) eve
Dutch (Holland).	Week	Zondag	Maandag	Dingsdag	Woensdag	Donderdag	Vrijdag	Zaturdag (Saturday).
Modern Friesian.	Wike	Snein	Moandel	Tlsdei	Wansdel	Thungersdel	Freedei	Snlund *Corruption* of Sonnabend.
English (England).	Week	Sunday	Monday	Tuesday	Wednesday	Thursday	Friday	Saturday Saturn-day.
Icelandic (Iceland).	Vika	Sunnudagur	Manudagur	Thridhjudagur	Midhvikudagur	Fimmtudagur	Fostudagur	Laugardagur (Of-bathday).
Swedish. Sweden.	Vecka	Sondag	Mandag	Tisdag	Onsdag	Thorsdag	Fredag	Lordag *Corruption* of Icelandic, laugardagur.

136   SABBATH AND SUNDAY.

	Uge	Sondag	Mandag	Tirsdag	Onsdag	Torsdag	Fredag	Loverdag *Corruption of Icelandic laugardagur.*
Danish. (Denmark).								
Old Slave Bulgaria. (d.)	Sedmica, Sedmina	Nedjelja, Voskresenie	Ponedjelnik	Vtornik	Sreda	Tshetverg, Tshetvertok	Pjatok	Subbota (Sabbath).
Russian (Russia).	Nedjelja	Voskresenje	Ponedjelnik	Vtornik	Sereda	Tshetvertok	Pjatnica	Subbota (Sabbath).
Illyrian (Dalmatia Servia).	Nedjelja	Nedjelja	Ponedeljak	Utorak, Vtornik	Srieda	Tshetvriak	Petak	Subota (Sabbath).
New Slovenian. Illyria, in Austria.	Teden, Tjeden Keden	Nedela	Ponedelek	Tork, Vtork	Sreda	Tshetertek	Petek	Sobota Sabbath.
Bulgarian (Bulgaria).	Nedjelja	Nedjelja	Ponedjelnik	Vtornik	Srjeda	Tshetvertak	Petak	Swbbota (Sabbath).
Polish (Poland).	Tydzienj, Niedziele, *pl.*	Niedziela	Ponledzialek	Wtorek	Sjroda	Czwartek	Piatek	Sobota (Sabbath).
Bohemian (Bohemia).	Tyden, Nedele, *pl.*	Nedele	Pondjelek	Uterek	Streda	Tshtvrtek	Patek	Sobota (Sabbath).

III.—JAPHETIC GROUP.—Concluded.

Lusatian (Saxony).	Tydzjenj, Njedzjele, *pl.*	Njedzjela	Pondzjela	Wutora	Srjeda	Shtwortk	Pjatk	Sobota (Sabbath).
Polabic. Borders of the Elbe. (d)	Nedelja	Nedelja	Pnedelja, Pnedilja, Pnedilj	Tory	Sreda	Perundan	Skopy	Subuta Sabbath.
Lithuanian (Prussian Lithuania).	Nedelia Nedele	Nedelia	Panedelis	Utarninkas	Sereda	Ketwergus	Petnyczja	Subata (Sabbath).
Prussian Prussia (d)		Nadele	Ponadele		Posissa-waite	Ketwirtire	Pentinx	Sabatico (Sabbath).
Lettish (Baltic Russia).	Neddela	Swedina	Pirmdina	Oridna	Treschdina	Zetturdi- na	Pikdina	Sesdina Sixth-day (of work)

IV.—ADDITIONAL USES.

The following table shows certain additional facts relative to the order of the days of the week in ordinary practical affairs. Indeed, an ordinary almanac is sufficient to refute many of the objections that are raised against the order of the week, and the identity of the Sabbath.

Week	Dominica	Feria Secunda	Feria Tertia	Feria Quarta	Feria Quinta	Feria Sexta	Sabbatum
Ecclesiastical							
Parliamentary	Dies Solis	Dies Lunæ	Dies Martis	Dies Mercurii	Dies Jovis	Dies Veneris	Dies Sabbati
Calendrical	Sunday	Monday	Tuesday	Wednesday	Thursday	Friday	Saturday
English Bible	The First Day	The Second Day	The Third Day	The Fourth Day	The Fifth Day	The Sixth Day	The Seventh Day, and the Sabbath

In the same order the Astronomical use proceeds by using the sign of the Sun for the first day and that of Saturn for the last day. The same order prevails in all business and social life, and has prevailed throughout the Christian Era, just as it had prevailed previous to Christ. Under such an array of evidence, presumption and ignorance could scarcely go farther than to assert that the order of the week, and the identity of the Sabbath are not well known, and thoroughly established.

The testimony of the *seventy-five* languages and dialects, given in the preceding tables, links the weeks and the Sabbath as they have come to us in an unbroken chain through the historic period. The nations that spoke many of these languages have long since gone from the earth. But the words of their mother tongue embalm their thoughts and practices as ineffaceable and unmistakable monuments showing the identity of the week and of the Sabbath. Tides of emigration have swept hither and thither over the earth. Empires have risen, flourished, and fallen, but the *week* has endured, amid all convulsions and changes. The earth as whirled upon its axis, and all longitudinal difficulties which some men now assert as against the identity of the days and the week, have existed since man began his course of empire over the earth. Humanity has belted the globe, in its progress, whether from one or from both ways, it matters not, and ages have failed to produce that confusion which superficial thinkers ignorantly assert. In this table of days philology has done for the truth concerning God's eternal Sabbath, what cuneiform inscriptions, and mummy pits, are doing for general and national history. When the facts presented in these appendices are given a fair consideration, cavil must cease, whatever practice as to the Sabbath the reader may continue to pursue. God's Sabbath, the busy day of modern life, and the sneered-at relic of Judaism, is here shown to be one of the great facts in universal history. Your duty to observe it, hereafter, dear reader, must rest upon the light now before you. God measures our duty by present knowledge, and not by past opportunities. May the Lord grant you strength to follow the way of right and righteousness

GENERAL INDEX.

	PAGE.
Alford, on Matthew xxviii. 1; and on Luke xxiii. 54,	56
A priori argument,	1–4
Brown, Prof. Francis, Sabbath and cuneiform inscriptions,	93
Calendar, European from Roman	112
Calendar, Roman under Numa,	112
Calendar, Roman under Julius,	113
Calendar, changed by Gregory XIII.,	114
Chambers' Cyc., origin of the week	98
Change-of-day theory, Illogical,	47
" " Propositions examined,	47
Christ, the central point in both dispensations,	23
Christ did not teach the abrogation of the Decalogue,	23
Christ's example concerning the Sabbath,	26
Christ kept Sabbath not simply as a Jew,	33
Christ's example concerning Sunday.	64
Christ, resurrection of, prophecy concerning	50
Christ's resurrection not on Sunday,	59
Christ's crucifixion and entombment, on Fourth day of the week,	59
Christ rose on the Seventh day of the week,	59
Christ, an impostor, if he did not lie in the grave three days and three nights,	63
Christ, resurrection of, Matthew's account	53
Christ, resurrection of, Mark's account	53
Christ, resurrection of, Luke's account	52

INDEX.

	PAGE.
Christ, resurrection of, John's account	52
"Collection," at Troas, *private*	81
Covenant, definition of	15
Covenant, word first used,	15
Covenant, deeper meaning of	16
Covenant, under the "new," God's law is written in the heart; passages referred to, Heb. x. 16; 2 Cor. iii.; Rom. 1st to 7th chap.	17
Covenant, under the "old," salvation came through ceremonies; under the "new," through faith in Christ,	21
Days, table of, great value of	122
Decalogue, the, composed of primary, unchangeable laws,	13
Decalogue, the, basis of the Hebrew theocracy	13
Decalogue, the, abrogation of, would destroy the gospel of Christ,	21
Decalogue, the, was the foundation of both covenants,	21
Edkins, Joseph, Chinese week,	110
Emmaus, Christ's walk to, after his resurrection,	61
Epistles contain only one mention of Sunday,	81
Goguet, Pres., primeval week,	110
Jones, Rev. Wm. M., table of days, etc.,	120
Lange, Trans. of John xx. 19—23,	65
Law, definition of	1
Law, primary, not abrogable	1
Law antedates creation and moral government	1
Law of the Sabbath, primary,	2
Law of the Sabbath, universal and unchangeable,	3
Law of the Sabbath, operative at man's creation,	5
Longitude and the Sabbath,	114
Lord's day, Rev. i. 10.	86
Luke notes customary acts,	74

INDEX.

	PAGE.
Manna, the gathering of, a test of Sabbath observance,	11
Meyer, on 1 Cor. xvi. 2,	83
Muller, Prof. Max, Hindu week, etc.,	107
No-Sabbathism defined,	36
No-Sabbathism, claims of, examined, from Old Testament.	37
No-Sabbathism from New Testament,	39
No-Sabbathism, fruitage of, only evil,	45
No-Sabbathism, passages examined, Deut. v. 2, 3, 15,	37
No-Sabbathism, passages examined, Ex. xx. 2; Lev. xxvi. 13; Psa. lxxxi. 9, 10, etc.,	38
No-Sabbathism, passages examined, Rom. xiv. 1—7,	39
No-Sabbathism, passages examined, Rom. vii. 12,	41
No-Sabbathism, passages examined, James ii. 10,	42
No-Sabbathism, passages examined, Col. ii. 16, 17,	42
No-Sabbathism, passages examined, 2 Cor. iii. 7, 8,	44
No-Sabbathism, passages examined, Rom. v. 13,.	45
No-Sabbathism makes infidelity better than belief,	45
No-Sabbathism *makes rejection of Christ the only means of salvation,*	45
Oppert, on cuneiform inscriptions,	96
Paul teaches the perpetuity of the Decalogue,	25
Paul kept the Sabbath while establishing Christian churches,	27
Pentecost, Acts ii. 1, not on Sunday,	70
Pentecost, why Holy Spirit then given.	72
Philological museum, Saturn's day indentical with the Sabbath,	105
Philological argument, importance of	119
Proctor, Prof. R. A., origin of week, etc.,	99
Readings, various. on 1 Cor. xvi. 2,	81
Reasons for choosing the Seventh day,	2
Rotherham, translation of John xx. 19—23,	65
Sabbath idea first expressed in the rest of Jehovah,	2
Sabbath law and Sabbath-day inseparable,	5

INDEX

	PAGE.
Sabbath-day and Seventh-day inseparable,	6
Sabbath institution the result of obedience to the Sabbath law,	7
Sabbath, known before the giving of the Decalogue,	8
Sabbath law not ceremonial,	13
Sabbath not "Jewish,"	32
Sabbath mentioned 60 times in the New Testament,	33
Sabbath *Memorial, The*	120
Sayce, A. H., Chaldean Sabbath,	96
Smith, C. Geo., Accadian Sabbath,	96
Sunday observance, John xx. 26, (?)	69
Sunday observance in book of Acts, (?)	70
Sunday, Paul traveled on, from Troas,	78
Troas, meeting at, held on evening after the Sabbath,	77
Tyndale, on 1 Cor. xvi. 2,	82
Week, origin of	96
Week, Babylonian	91
Week, Accadian	91
Week, Indian	105
Week, identity of	119
Week, in Semitic languages,	124
Week, known to Patriarchs,	10
Week, Hebrew, unbroken as to succession,	90
Week, Chinese	109
Week, in Hamitic languages,	126
Week, in Japhetic languages,	126
Wilson, H. H., origin of the week,	106

www.ingramcontent.com/pod-product-compliance
Lightning Source LLC
Chambersburg PA
CBHW022126160426
43197CB00009B/1167